USBORNE
ECONOMICS
FOR BEGINNERS

Written by Lara Bryan and Andy Prentice

Illustrated by Federico Mariani

Economics experts: David Stallibrass and Pedro Serôdio

Designed by Jamie Ball and Freya Harrison

Contents

Chapter 1: Not enough to go around   13

The things we need to survive, how we choose them,
and why there's never enough time: the big reasons why
economies exist.

Chapter 2: Markets   23

Buying and selling and how prices are set –
as if by magic.

Chapter 3: Making choices   37

How do people make choices and why are those choices
often unexpected? How can businesses and governments
change people's choices? Why would they want to?

Chapter 4: Production, profit and competition   51

What big choices do businesses face? Why is competition so
important? Why do some businesses produce pollution and
what should we do about it?

Chapter 5: Economic systems   67

Is there a set of rules that would make it possible to share
everything fairly? Or is it better to have winners and losers?
What systems have people tried?

Usborne Quicklinks

For links to websites where you can find out more about economics,
from supply and demand to price bubbles and globalization, with video
clips, games, activities and quizzes, go to the Usborne Quicklinks website at
Usborne.com/Quicklinks and type in the title of this book.

Here are some of the things you can do at Usborne Quicklinks:

- Play games to control inflation or manage the national debt
- Try test-yourself quizzes on economic terms
- Watch video clips on trade, markets and more

Please follow the internet safety guidelines at the Usborne
Quicklinks website. Children should be supervised online.

What is economics?

Some people think that economics is all about money, banks and very complicated graphs. But it's actually a lot simpler than that – much of economics is really about **understanding choices**.

Imagine there are two chocolate and two pineapple cupcakes. There's enough for four of you to have one cupcake each. How do you share them out?

Now you and your friends are going to have to make a choice about who gets what.

There's never enough for everyone to get what they want. So people have to **make choices** about how to share in a way that makes them happy.

This is what **economics** is all about.

When there isn't enough of something, it's **scarce**. Scarcity is an important idea in economics – it's what forces people to make choices. You might be surprised how often you make choices about things that are scarce.

Ketchup could be scarce.

For most people, money is scarce.

Even *time* is scarce.

What is an economy?

When a group of people is making choices about what to do, buy or sell it creates an **economy**. An economy can be very small or really big, depending on the number of people making choices.
An economy is created by...

...a group of people living under one roof.

> I'll mop the floor if you do the dishes.

...the people living or working in a town or city.

> Should I drive or take the bus to go to work?

> All our concert tickets are sold out!

> If we spend more money on city parks, there will be less to give to schools.

> Should we open another shop?

A BIG economy, such as the economy of a country or the world, is a network made up of lots of *smaller* economies – all the households, villages, towns and cities within it.

What do economists study?

Economists are the people that study economies. Some focus on individuals or small groups, while others zoom out to look at the bigger picture. And some economists end up asking – and trying to answer – some surprising questions...

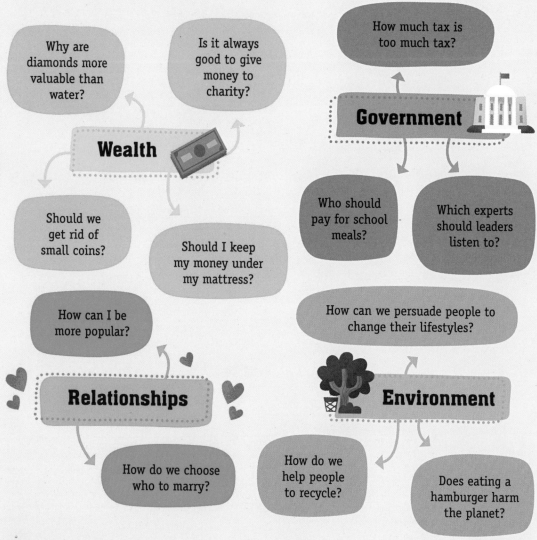

Why are diamonds more valuable than water?

Is it always good to give money to charity?

How much tax is too much tax?

Wealth

Government

Should we get rid of small coins?

Should I keep my money under my mattress?

Who should pay for school meals?

Which experts should leaders listen to?

How can I be more popular?

How can we persuade people to change their lifestyles?

Relationships

Environment

How do we choose who to marry?

How do we help people to recycle?

Does eating a hamburger harm the planet?

Economics for good

By finding answers to all these questions, economists hope to encourage people, businesses and governments to make better choices – and, hopefully, make the world a better, fairer place. Economics isn't about labeling people or governments as "good" or "bad" – it's about observing the choices that people make and trying to understand why they've made them.

Should *everyone* have a job?

At what age should people stop working?

What's the best time to rob a bank?

Are people who work longer hours more productive?

Work

Crime

Why are women often paid less than men?

Why does poverty breed crime?

Is putting criminals in prison a good idea?

Why do some businesses have January sales?

 Businesses

How expensive is having a child?

 **Families**

Are big businesses dangerous?

How can I sell more of my product?

How can I trust someone in another country?

Is it better to leave home or live with your parents?

Does free trade make the world richer?

Sports

Trade

Do crowds affect the outcome of games?

Is there such a thing as a hot scoring streak?

Does it matter if children make my shoes?

The future

Can we eliminate poverty?

Will robots take my job?

Would mining on Mars fix the world economy?

How do you *do* economics?

Why do people make certain choices? What are the consequences of those choices? To investigate these kinds of questions, economists usually start by coming up with an explanation, or **model**.

Here's a question

The rice crop is very bad this year. It's the staple food for more than half the world's population. What will happen?

NEWS NOW

Here's a model

When there's a shortage, prices rocket and lots of people will suffer.

Modeling

A model is a simplified way of explaining how something works – in this case the relationship between quantity and price. Economists often show models using graphs, instead of words.

Price

New price
Old price

Quantity

This looks complicated, but it's just the same as what I said above – using math!

Models can be helpful for making predictions, or **forecasts**.

You're predicting that the price of rice in stores will increase by about 30%.

NEWS NOW

Governments should prepare stocks of food to give to those most in need.

Test it out

Economists can test a model by collecting information, or **data**, and seeing whether it matches the model or not.

The model was pretty accurate. This helped governments put the right plan in place.

The Newspaper

GOVERNMENTS HAND OUT RICE PACKAGES

Governments rationing rice

Economics is an argument

Even though all economists study data – sometimes exactly the same data – they often come to different conclusions about what it's saying.

Rice rations prevented many families from starving! It's really good that the government took control of the situation.

I think rationing made no difference. Over time, prices would've gone down without government interference.

Just like everyone else, economists often have different ideas about how societies *should* work, or a different sense of what's fair. Even in this book, the way we describe economics and the examples we've chosen show our **biases** – the things *we* think are important. Here are some different ways of seeing the world. You might strongly agree or disagree with some of them.

The world is too unequal. It's not fair that anyone is richer than anyone else.

I think big businesses are bad! They make so much money because they can push smaller companies out of the way.

I think big businesses are good! They only become rich and successful if they're better than their competitors.

There are economists to back up all of these opinions.

British economist
Joan Robinson once said...

The purpose of studying economics is to learn how to avoid being deceived by economists.

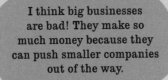

Chapter 1:
Not enough to go around

If everyone could have anything they wanted, at any time, with no effort needed to get it – there probably wouldn't be any economists. But the world we live in isn't like that.

Every day, everyone must make choices about how to keep on living in a world where **resources** such as food, materials and energy are **scarce** and everyone's time is limited. Studying this challenge is the fundamental task of economics.

The challenge of survival

Our need for food, water, and shelter hasn't changed since our earliest ancestors walked the Earth. Economists talk about us using up, or **consuming**, the Earth's resources to fulfill these needs.

Let's have a look at some of the resources our distant ancestors consumed...

Shelter

Wood

Flint

Animal skins

Meat

Medicine

Fish

Fruit

Water

Mushrooms

On some days, getting these resources might have been pretty easy. But you can be sure that there were other days when resources were scarce.

Everything around us is a potential resource. Modern economies consume many *different* kinds of resources in ways that our ancestors didn't – not just things to eat, drink or use as tools. Here are some of them...

Sunshine

Manure

Oil

Uranium

Sand

Wind

The cost of choice

Every choice has a cost even if you don't pay money for it. This is because any choice you make makes other choices impossible. Economists call this an **opportunity cost.** The cost to you is all the other things that you chose *not to do* instead.

Most resources can only be used once. The *opportunity cost* of consuming a resource is all the other ways you might have used that resource.

Your time is scarce too. If you spend time doing one thing, that means you've chosen not to spend time doing other things. That's an opportunity cost too.

Frequently, it is very hard to know what the right choice is. You might have to choose between what you want and what you need, or between a short-term gain and a long-term benefit.

To make a choice, people often weigh up how much benefit they will get. Economists call this **utility**.

The utility of something varies from person to person.

People are complicated, so they may make some interesting decisions. Lots of different factors go into deciding what gives you the most utility.

The safest option was to run away, but the girl decided to risk her life to save her dad. Luckily for him, she thought a living dad benefitted her the most.

Turning resources into products

Sometimes we use resources to make other things. This is called **production**. Economists usually break down the process of production into four main parts.

1) In order to produce something, you first need an **idea**. What do you want to make and how do you want to make it?

2) Then you need **resources**.

3) Economists call the work you have to put into producing something **labor**.

Labor isn't just the manual effort that goes into making something, but all the other work too. This includes thinking up ideas and leadership. Anything that takes time is labor.

4) Tools and technology help us to work faster, better or more safely – in other words more efficiently. Economists call these things **capital**.

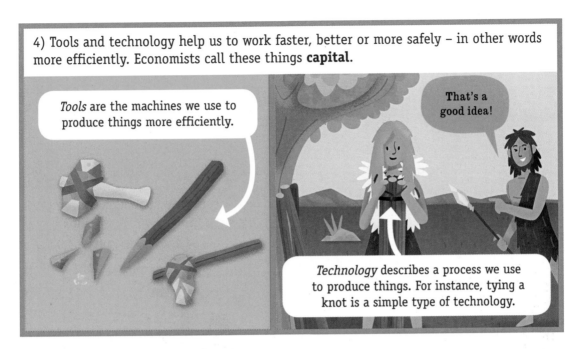

This is how production works.

Production = idea + resources + labor + capital

New ideas, tools or technology make people more **productive**. This means making more things more efficiently. Economists study productivity because it helps improve people's lives – thanks to the wall, the family is now safer.

From resources to economies

Imagine you had to make everything you needed to survive yourself. Then imagine everyone else having to do the same. It wouldn't be very efficient. This is why it makes sense to divide up most tasks.

Economists call this division of tasks **specialization**.

Some people specialize in gathering or producing **goods**.

Some people specialize in doing things for others. These jobs are known as **services**.

When people spend a lot of time specializing in just one job, they become more efficient. They often invent new technologies and get faster at producing things.

> I do all the sewing around here. I can make two shirts in under an hour now.

> I'm good at inventing things. My latest creation is called a... **DOOR**!

People who specialize in a task usually produce more of a good or service than they need for themselves. This extra production is known as a **surplus**.

> I've got more fish than I can eat. What should I do with them?

Surpluses are vital to the economy. People can exchange or **trade** their surplus with each other to get all the other things they need.

When you exchange goods directly like this it's known as **bartering**.

Today, we tend to trade using money.

Specialization and trade are the foundation of all **economies**, no matter how big or small. That's how it was thousands of years ago, and it's still like that today.

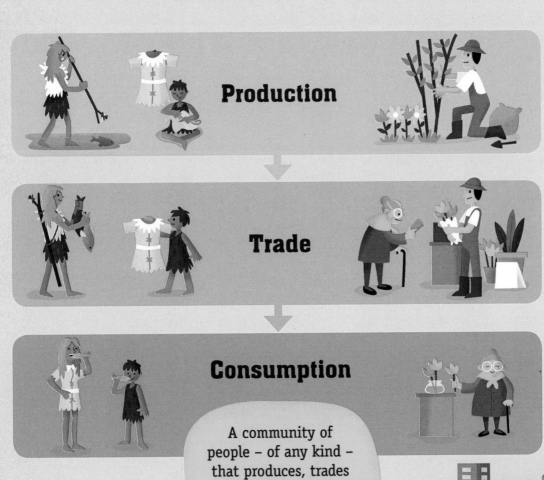

Production

Trade

Consumption

A community of people – of any kind – that produces, trades and consumes is **an economy**.

Chapter 2: Markets

Everything people do – from making ice cream to performing surgery – depends on exchanges of knowledge, goods, services and ideas. A place where people meet to exchange things is known as a **market**.

Over the centuries, economists have analyzed all sorts of markets and discovered various patterns that describe how they work. They've also put forward ideas on how to make sure people trade fairly and efficiently.

Making, buying and selling

All the making, selling and buying in an economy allows people to get the things they want and need. It sounds simple, but at every stage of the process something magical happens – *value* gets created.

Take this rock, around 2,000 years ago...

Making something out of the rock adds value to it.

Trading the statue creates value, too.

For the *seller*, the value is the difference between the price and the cost of making the product.

Price: 40 coins
Cost: 15 coins (tools + time spent)

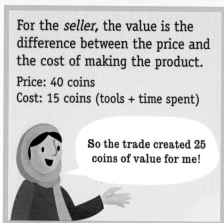

For the *buyer*, the value is harder to measure. It's the difference between the utility the buyer gets from the purchase and the price paid.

For trading to work, both sides need to believe they're gaining something. They also need to **trust** the other person to supply the promised goods or pay the agreed amount of money.

However much people need each other's goods and services, if they can't *find* each other, trade won't happen. This is the origin of the **market**. The Greek *agora*, the Chinese *shìchâng*, or this Persian *šūqā* are all examples of ancient markets.

Markets bring buyers and sellers together.

I've told all my friends to come and find you here.

AZAR'S ART EMPORIUM

Buyers and sellers exchange things for a price.

A bowl of stew for one coin!

ZZZ ZZZ ZZZ

DELICIOUS STEW!

People have different opinions on what that price should be.

2 coins

I **love** this hat.

Mmm, yes but I'm not sure it's worth 2 coins.

Who'll buy my bull?

High utility

Low utility

Ten coins!

Twenty coins!

FIFTY coins!

SHEEP! 15 COINS

This buyer wants the bull more, so is willing to pay a higher price for it.

Those sheep are a bargain!

Maybe it is for you, but I can't afford it.

Wanting something isn't enough. The buyer also needs to be able to pay for it.

Many, many markets

As well as marketplaces with stalls, there are all kinds of markets around you. This scene shows six examples of everyday markets.

MR. SWISH WATCHES

OPEN

Scientists say this model should work even on the Moon.

Wow!

Should I buy these shoes?

Go for it!

St. Anna's School
est. 1986

It's my first day on the job.

Good luck!

They'll take a while to arrive. They're being shipped from Canada.

Can I have that card? I'll give you this one in exchange.

But this one's the captain. He's worth more!

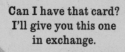

OK, I'll throw in a snack bar, too.

Deal!

A **shop** is a marketplace.

A market can be an online space such as a **website** or **app**, which connects buyers and sellers worldwide.

In the **informal market** for sports stickers, the buyer paid with a snack bar and a card instead of money.

A **workplace**, such as a school, is also a market, where people exchange their work for a salary.*

A stock exchange is a place where people buy and sell parts of companies, known as **stocks,** through a computer. The market for stocks is called the **stock market**.

If things are bought or sold illegally, it's known as a **black market**.

*Well, the teachers do. The children have to work and don't get paid. Is that fair?

Supply and demand

If you look at any market, you'll notice that the amount people want to sell or buy – known as **supply and demand** – usually follows certain patterns. Economists call these patterns the **laws of supply and demand**.

See if you can spot the pattern in this market for sandwiches of the same quality, but different prices.

More people want to buy the cheaper sandwiches and fewer people want to buy the expensive ones. That's because the lower the price, the more people think it is worth buying it.

Economists show the relationship between price and demand on a graph like this:

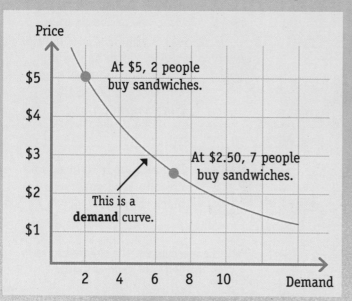

Law of demand

The higher the price, the lower the demand is. The lower the price, the higher the demand is.

The amount people are willing to **supply** also changes depending on the price, or reward. Take this poetry competition – more poems were submitted in the year with the higher reward.

A higher reward, or price, encourages more poets to supply poems. This graph shows the relationship between price and supply:

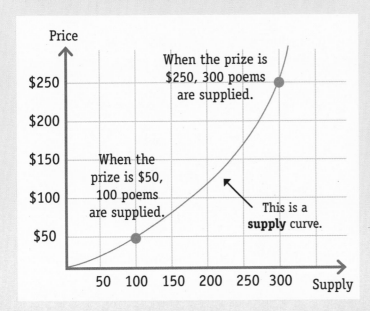

When the prize is $250, 300 poems are supplied.

When the prize is $50, 100 poems are supplied.

This is a **supply** curve.

Law of supply

The higher the price, the more supply there is. The lower the price, the less supply there is.

How prices respond to people

Prices influence how much people want to buy and produce. But it also works the other way around – how much people buy and produce makes prices change too.

If there's more supply than there is demand, it sends a signal to a seller to lower prices.

If there's less supply than there is demand, it sends a signal to a seller to increase prices.

Over time, the price changes until it reaches a point where there's as much demand as there is supply. This is known as the **equilibrium price**.

The price is just right – it's high enough for the seller, and low enough for customers. It also means there's no wasted mangoes.

In this kind of market, no one person is responsible for making the price change. It's the result of all the decisions made by buyers and sellers seeking to make a living and get the best deal. Here's how economists have tried to make sense of this process.

In the 18th-century, Scottish economist Adam Smith, described this process as the **invisible hand** of the market.

Without anyone giving orders, the market works out what people want and gets it to them.

About a century later, British economist Alfred Marshall developed Smith's idea of the invisible hand.

Supply and demand work *together* to set prices, just like a pair of blades cutting paper.

Marshall came up with the idea of showing the way supply and demand work *together* on a graph.

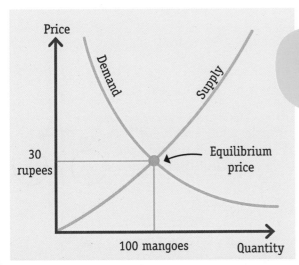

Price

Demand

Supply

30 rupees

Equilibrium price

100 mangoes

Quantity

There's a point where the demand curve meets the supply curve, which is called the equilibrium price. At this price, demand *equals* supply.

Changing markets

Supply and demand don't just change because of prices. Take bicycles – there are all sorts of reasons why the demand and supply of bikes might change...

Trends

Demand

People are trying to live healthier lifestyles, so *demand* for cycling is going up.

Costs of making

If the price of electricity goes up, it will cost more to make the bike, so *supply* is likely to go down.

Supply

Other prices

Demand

If bus tickets get more expensive, more people might switch to cycling. So *demand* goes up.

BUS TICKET
1 X RIDE
$100

Demand

Weather

If it's cold, the *demand* for cycling is likely to go down.

Number of suppliers

If a new bike shop opens, the *supply* of bikes will go up.

Supply

OPEN   OPEN

It's hard to tell, looking at all these changes, if the overall demand and supply of bikes has gone up or down. This makes it tricky for businesses to manage supply and demand.

I don't know whether to make more bikes or less.

How much change?

Some things respond more to changes than others. Imagine what would happen to the demand for bread and bikes if their prices doubled.

The demand for bread would drop but not by much. It's big part of people's diets, so they will continue to buy it. Demand is said to be **inelastic**.

The demand for bikes would drop by a lot. People don't need to buy bikes every day, so they're likely to put off the purchase. The demand is said to be **elastic**.

Businesses often work out how sensitive their customers are to changes in prices before making a decision about changing them.

Market model

A **model** is an explanation for how something works. The laws of supply and demand are models: they provide a simple explanation for the complicated process of how prices are set. *Real life* is usually not as smooth as models suggest – for example, it can take time for buyers and sellers to respond to each other's signals. But the laws are still useful, because they help to explain all sorts of situations...

Why is there traffic outside schools at certain times?

Because the *demand* for using a road is higher when parents are dropping off and collecting their kids than the *supply* of space on that road.

Why is a **SMALL** apartment in the city more expensive than a **BIG** house in the countryside?

There's a higher *demand* for housing in cities, but a lower *supply*. So the price of space is higher in the city than in the countryside.

The model even helps to solve problems.

How do you help young people find jobs?

The government could try to increase the *demand* for young workers, by giving money to companies who invest in training them.

How do you get people to use fewer plastic bags?

One way is to charge customers for bags. Many countries have tried this and seen a huge drop in *demand* as a result.

Fixing markets

In any market, businesses sell things to people who can afford them. This might *sound* reasonable, but it's not always fair, safe or even practical to put into practice. When this happens, it's known as **market failure**. The government often steps in at this point.

FAILURE

When there's a **shortage** of something, the price goes up and up. This is a disaster for anyone who can't afford it – especially if it's something essential such as water.

FAILURE

Schools and firefighters are **important** services but lots of people wouldn't be able to afford them if they had to pay for them.

FIX

In a drought, the government might decide to give everyone a certain amount of water for free every day.

Free water. No more than 2 bottles per day per person.

FIX

Governments often provide these things for everyone, whether they can pay for them or not.

FAILURE

When a business is the main or only supplier of a resource, it gives it a huge amount of **power** over consumers.

$500

$500 for a pair of shoes? That's ridiculous!

Tough! You've got no choice, I'm the only seller around.

FIX

Governments set rules to protect customers of very big companies, and also to stop businesses from getting too powerful. See more on page 60.

FAILURE

It's **impractical** to charge people individually for some resources such as streetlights. This means businesses can't make money from providing them.

FIX

So governments tend to provide them for everybody.

FAILURE

Producing and consuming sometimes have negative **side effects** that nobody pays for, such as pollution from a car factory.

FIX

One solution is a pollution tax, to encourage the factory to find a way to reduce its pollution.

> Buying a filter to clean the air coming out of the chimney would be cheaper than paying the tax.

Find out more about this kind of market failure on pages 64-65.

FAILURE

Sellers often **know more** about a product than consumers, so it's easy for consumers to get caught out.

NEARLY NEW

FIX

5 YEARS OLD

Governments can set rules to make businesses share information about a product.

FAILURE

If people want something enough, there will be a business willing to supply it, no matter how **dangerous** that thing is to the buyer or other people.

FIX

The government might restrict who can buy dangerous things such as fireworks.

+18s only

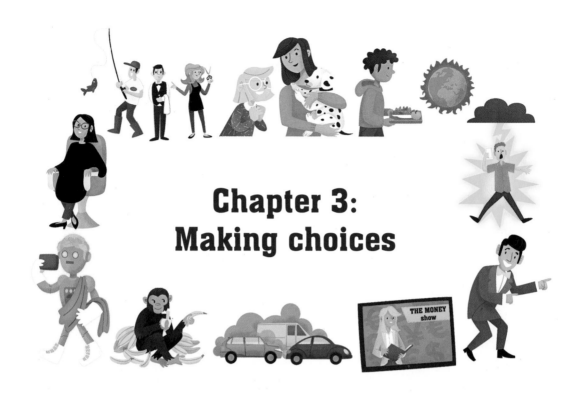

Chapter 3:
Making choices

Some economists like to use simplified **models** to make it easier to understand the messy reasons behind human choices. These models usually assume that people behave selfishly to get the most utility they can. The market models in the previous chapter work this way.

Since the 1970s, however, other economists have tried to explain the mess, in order to understand how people *actually* make choices. They believe that people are often illogical, badly informed and full of superstitions and biases. This field is known as **behavioral economics**.

Model behavior

Many useful economic theories are based on the idea that people consider each choice carefully and always seek out the most utility. To illustrate this, economists use a model called **Homo economicus**, which means "economic man" in Latin, the language of ancient Rome.

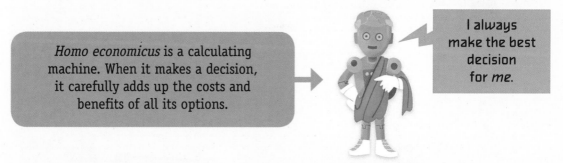

Homo economicus is a calculating machine. When it makes a decision, it carefully adds up the costs and benefits of all its options.

I always make the best decision for *me*.

What would happen if *Homo economicus* found a wallet in the street?

Options:
1. Keep wallet
2. Leave wallet
3. Find original owner

1 = gain stolen money, risk of feeling guilty

2 = easiest option, no risk

3 = takes time but feels like the right thing to do.

I think I'll just leave it.

Economists know that such precise analysis is not how most people make every decision. But they believe that it can accurately predict how a large number of people, on average, will make choices.

A few economists even argue that *all* our decisions, however small, are based on a selfish calculation – how much each of us personally stands to gain.

What do I gain from giving a wallet back to a stranger?

Isn't that totally unselfish?

I think it *is* selfish – you're choosing the action that makes you feel good..

Or maybe, you hate feeling guilty.

Ultra-selfish?

Behavioral economists think using *Homo economicus* to explain every choice is unrealistic. They use tests to show how people aren't actually thinking selfishly all the time. One famous test is known as the Ultimatum Game:

Frank is acting like a true *Homo economicus,* as he would get to keep the maximum amount of $99 with his $1 offer. If Nancy were just as money obsessed, she would *accept* his offer too. After all, having $1 is better than having $0.

However, test after test has shown that while playing the Ultimatum Game, proposers usually offer far more than $1, and responders often reject offers as high as $40. For many people it is more important to behave fairly, and to be treated fairly, than to gain any money at all.

The Ultimatum Game has even been played with chimpanzees. The chimps displayed a similar desire for fairness as humans did.

Whether it's the promise of a reward or the threat of punishment, *anything* that motivates you to make a choice is an **incentive**.

Some incentives come from other people, society or the government.

Money is a common incentive. People are incentivized to do a job by their salary.

The threat of prison can be a powerful incentive not to commit crimes.

Good exam results are an incentive to study hard.

Some incentives are personal. A way to understand is to ask: what motivates me?

The money's nice, but mostly I take pride in finishing a job.

I'm loyal to my friends, so I chose to go to prison rather than rat them out.

I just love reading books.

Everyone must decide how to balance out these different incentives. For example, some people might prefer a well-paid, boring job. Others might want a job that was less secure, but more entertaining or rewarding.

Influencing choices

Governments and businesses use incentives all the time to try to influence people's choices. Here are some examples.

Coffee shop loyalty cards reward returning customers.

Celebrity endorsements are an incentive to buy a product for people who admire that celebrity.

The government could raise taxes on businesses to make polluting more expensive. This incentivizes the use of greener technologies.

A government that wanted to encourage new technologies to be developed could set up prizes to reward inventors.

THE NEWS

FUSION GENIUS SCOOPS PRIZE!!!

Governments that use incentives to change behavior have to be very careful. When incentives are poorly designed, they may not change behavior in the way they were intended.

Blood donation is a very important part of modern medicine, but it is often hard to get enough donors to step forward.

...but several studies have shown that when blood donors are paid, blood donation actually goes down.

Give blood and get $50!

Oh no, I wouldn't do it for money.

You might think that *paying* people to give blood would encourage more donations...

For most people, the incentive for donating blood is the satisfaction of a kind, charitable act. This feeling was undermined when payment became the main incentive for donation.

So how *do* we make choices?

Imagine that you want an ice cream. You might think carefully through a whole range of decisions.

Cone?
Bar?
Tub?

How far to travel?
10 minutes for OK ice cream?
Half an hour for good?
An hour for the best?

What flavor is best?
Chocolate, strawberry, vanilla, cherry, banana, mint, fudge, cookie dough, rocky road...

How many scoops?
2, 4, 9?!!

Woah!
Too much!

Isn't it too cold for ice cream?

Do you actually want frozen yogurt?

Hot chocolate sauce?
Sprinkles?
Chocolate chips?

How much do I want to spend? A lot? A little?

What about spoiling my dinner?

Now imagine that you went through the same process for every choice you made. You'd never get anything done!

This is why, usually, people don't reason out their choices. They rely instead on simple **rules of thumb** to make their choice quickly, without thinking about it too much at all.

I'll have vanilla in a cone. I always have vanilla in a cone and I like it.

It's more efficient to make choices fast – but there is a cost. Behavioral economists have identified many biases that creep into quick thinking. Biases affect the choices that people make, but they aren't necessarily bad.

Availability bias

People tend to choose the easiest thing – or the first thing they can think of.

Similarity bias

People tend to go for a choice that fits with what they've experienced or seen before.

Herding

People feel more comfortable making the same decision as other people.

Bias in action

Herding can cause **price bubbles**, when everyone tries to buy the same thing at the same time. This causes the price to rise dramatically.

It can also lead to **price crashes**, when everyone tries to sell the same thing at the same time. Find out what can happen after a crash on page 84.

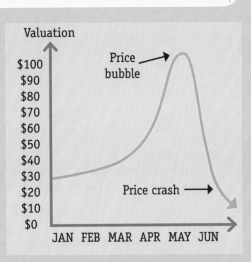

Human judgement

Some biases are present even when people believe they're carefully considering every option before making a choice. For example...

Once people own something, they tend to overvalue it.

This is known as the endowment effect.

People overestimate the likelihood of unlikely events.

You are roughly 150 times more likely to be hit by lightning than to win a lottery jackpot.

People tend to overestimate the ability of experts to make predictions about the future.

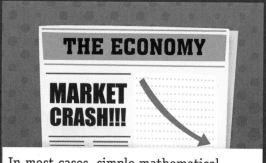

In most cases, simple mathematical models perform better than humans at making predictions.

People's choices are also hugely affected by *how* information about their choices is presented to them. This is known as **framing bias**. Sellers use this all the time to get customers to spend more money.

POPS $3.99 — Most popular

Pam's $4.99

When offered the choice between two popcorn brands, two thirds of customers preferred the cheaper option, while one third chose the more expensive.

But when a third, higher-priced "decoy" option was added to the menu, 90% of people now chose to buy the middle-priced popcorn, even though it had been the most expensive before.

POPS $3.99

Pam's $4.99 — Most popular

PAPA P $5.50

By offering an expensive product as a distraction, businesses trick people into buying something only a little cheaper – and make you feel you are getting a better deal as well.

Nudging

There are (arguably) nicer ways that our biases can be used against us. By framing people's choices, you can also get them to make decisions that are better for them. This is known as **choice architecture**, or **nudging**.

In an experiment to help students eat healthier, economists found that they didn't need to ban junk food in a school. Instead, they realized that placing good, fresh food at eye level helped the students *choose* salads rather than their usual serving of fried food.

Risk

When you make a choice, there's a chance it won't turn out as you'd hoped. This is called a **risk**. For example, this person is weighing up the risks of a new haircut.

When people make choices they compare the risk to the potential reward.

My haircut	pixie cut	dye blonde	a little trim
My risk of regret	huge	medium	small
My reward	dream look	big change	safe

For this person, although the pixie cut was a big risk, the potential reward was too great to ignore.

The amount of risk you will tolerate is your individual choice. Some people and companies are risk-loving, while others avoid risks. But the prospect of a really big reward can sometimes tempt the most cautious to chase their dream.

How do you really feel about risk?

Although people always weigh up risks and rewards, they don't always do it in a consistent way. For example, people change their attitude to gambling depending on whether they are gaining or losing money.

Try this experiment:

Which of these boxes would you choose?

BOX A

WIN $900 FOR SURE!

BOX B

A 90% CHANCE TO WIN $1,000!

(10% CHANCE TO WIN NOTHING)

What about this time? Choose C or D.

BOX C

LOSE $900 FOR SURE

BOX D

A 90% CHANCE TO LOSE $1,000!

(10% CHANCE TO LOSE NOTHING)

Results

Most people choose the less risky Box A for the first game. When playing the second game, however, most people choose to take a bigger risk. In the hope of avoiding *any* loss, they gamble by choosing Box D.

People seem to *hate* losing much more than they *like* winning. So they are willing to take bigger risks to avoid it. This is why it can be more effective for governments to punish bad behavior than reward good behavior.

People really, *really* hate losing money.

Making group decisions

A group of people making choices that make sense for themselves can cause trouble when they all share a resource with each other.
Take this example of a sheep-farming village:

The villagers each graze their own herd of sheep on communal land.

The sheep grow fat and the villagers grow rich. They all buy more sheep.

No one thinks about the fact that grazing more of their own sheep will take away the grass from everyone else's sheep. The grass starts to run out.

BUMP

Soon there is no more grass, and no more sheep. Everyone loses out and the villagers become poor.

Bad outcomes like this do happen in the real world. When a group of people, towns or even entire countries share a resource, they often overexploit it. Economists call it the **tragedy of the commons**. Here are some examples.

Roads fill up when too many people drive to work so no one goes anywhere.

In the 20th century, North Atlantic cod supplies were almost wiped out by overfishing.

Countries make so much carbon dioxide, they're dangerously changing the Earth's atmosphere.

American economist Elinor Ostrom researched ways to prevent these kinds of situations. In 2009, she became the first woman to be awarded the Nobel Prize for Economics. Her solution was to get people talking.

Government laws that *force* people *not* to overexploit resources don't always work. Enforcing these laws is difficult, and many people ignore them.

Ostrom went around the world and studied communities where people had to share common resources.

She found that in places where neighbors all lived close to the resource, and talked to each other...

...they didn't overexploit it. The more people talked to their neighbors, the better they ran their communities.

Strong communities help their members make better choices. If people know and trust each other, and know how they are expected to behave, then they are less likely to behave selfishly.

But how can we save the entire planet? We can't be *neighbors* with seven billion people.

You're right, that's impossible.

But a good start is to work closely with our own communities. Now help me plant this tree!

Chapter 4:
Production, profit and competition

Most people buy what they want and need from other people or **businesses**. Businesses **compete** with each other to attract the most customers. A successful business makes more money than it spends. This is known as making a **profit**.

Business owners have to make all sorts of choices if they hope to compete successfully and make decent profits...

What do businesses do?

Businesses come in all shapes and sizes, but they all have this in common: they produce goods and services that people need or want, and they exchange what they produce for money.

All businesses spend money...

The money a business spends on producing and selling their product is known as a **cost**.

I have to buy wool, stuffing, cotton and glass to make my teddy bears.

MEGABEAR INCORPORATED

Once a cost has been paid for, it is known as a **sunk cost**.

Some costs are **variable** depending on how much of a product the business produces. If they produce more, these costs will go up.

Raw materials — Glass eyes

Wages

Warehouse space

Some costs are known as **fixed costs**, because they remain the same regardless, no matter how much of a product a business produces.

Rent

Debt

Managers

BUY ME! Advertising

...and try to make money too.

The money a business receives when it sells its product is its **revenue**.

We sold 100 chairs for $500 – so our revenue was $50,000.

All businesses want to make a profit

Profit is the money left over from a business' revenue, after all costs are paid. It's the incentive for all the risk and hard work involved in running a business.

revenues - costs = profit

All businesses face competition

In most markets, businesses must **compete** fiercely with each other to attract customers. They want customers to choose *their* product rather than a rival's.

Big and small

Every size of business has its advantages and disadvantages.

Small businesses...

...are easier to run because they are less complex.

What's our new idea this week?

...adapt quickly to changing markets.

Let's try using recycled material.

...can make highly specialized products to escape competition.

We can market a line of chairs made out of recycled cardboard!

JENNY'S CHAIRS

A drawback of small businesses is they often have to pay other businesses to do some things for them.

We have to pay another company to deliver our chairs.

We drive for MEGABEAR!

Big businesses...

...can produce and control everything they need themselves, from design to advertising and distribution – which can save a lot on costs.

This is because the more of something you produce, the cheaper it gets. It's one reason why big businesses can generate big profits. It happens because...

...more specialized workers and processes are more efficient.

...raw materials are cheaper in big quantities.

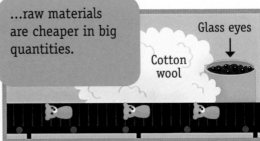

...fixed costs such as taxes and rent are spread out over more sales.

These are all known as **economies of scale.**

Is bigger always better?

After a certain point, expansion stops being worth it – costs begin to rise again and revenues fall. This is known as a **diseconomy of scale.** Some common problems for bigger companies are...

...they are hard to run and slow to change.

...different departments don't know what the others are doing.

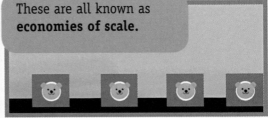

...workers in big companies can feel unappreciated and work less hard.

MEGABEAR, INC

Knowing when to stop

To make the biggest profit, you might think that every business would choose to produce as much of their product as possible. But as usual, it's not that simple.

Many businesses fail because they don't know when to stop getting bigger. To decide how much to produce, well-run businesses look at the cost and potential profit of producing just *one* more thing. Studying the next tiny step down the road like this is known as **marginal analysis**.

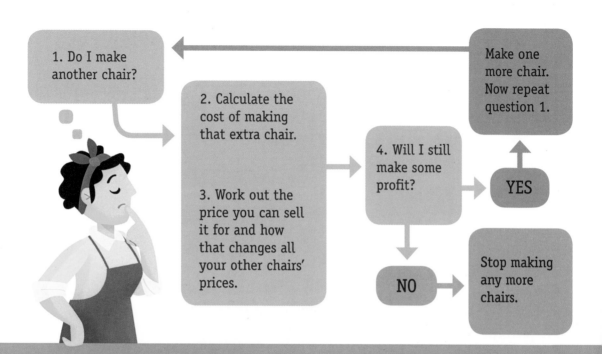

Every day, people make choices using marginal analysis, even if they don't realize it. For example: is it worth staying up an extra hour to play a new video game?

It's not just producers who make marginal decisions; consumers have to make them too. For example: is it worth eating one more burger?

Utility tends to go down the more you consume something. Eventually, having more stops being worth it, even if the price goes down.

Competition

Competition makes products cheaper for consumers and gives them more choice. It also makes the economy more efficient. Here's how a competitive market works:

If a business is doing well, it will tempt other businesses to try producing the same product or service.

Competing businesses often lower their prices to attract buyers. Now the original business has to lower *their* prices, because they will sell nothing if they overcharge. This is called **price competition**.

Another way of attracting clients is to offer a better service, or to be more efficient. By using resources better and wasting less, businesses can gain an advantage over their rivals.

The price for failure is steep. A business that is not competitive will not last long.

So how do you defend yourself from competitors? Escaping from price competition is what drives firms to try new ideas and sell better products:

Technology

By inventing a new technology, businesses can leave competition behind. For example, since the invention of the motor car, over 100 years ago, horse-powered transportation has declined.

Quality

By making a better product, a business can distinguish itself from its rivals. If a business has a reputation for high quality, it can charge higher prices.

Productivity

More productive businesses make things more quickly and cheaply than their rivals. Henry Ford did just that in 1913, when he invented the **assembly line...**

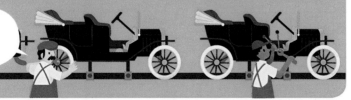

Advertising

People are more likely to buy something they've heard of. So businesses that reach out to customers by advertising are likely to do better – even though it costs money to advertise.

Competition encourages the development of new, exciting ideas and better-run businesses, but it can also lead to businesses shutting down. This process is known as **creative destruction**, and many governments help people who lose their jobs because of it.

Monopolies

Imagine you owned all the chocolate in the world. You could decide exactly how much to sell, and set the price too. When a business has complete control over a market like this, it's known as a **monopoly**.

In a monopoly there is no competition, which usually means fewer, less varied products and much higher prices. It is another example of a market failure.

Some monopolies are created by governments or laws. For example, in some countries only pharmacists or taxi drivers with a government license are allowed to operate.

Businesses can also create monopolies by buying up all their competitors.

But not all monopolies are bad. In some cases, they even make sense.

Imagine if eight water companies all wanted to lay pipes to supply water to your house.

Sometimes competition is inefficient or impossible. When this happens, it's called a **natural monopoly**. It's then up to the government to protect consumers to make sure they get a good deal.

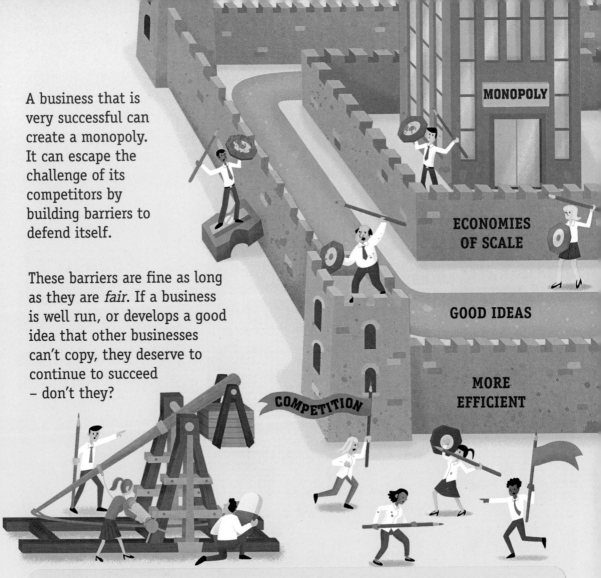

A business that is very successful can create a monopoly. It can escape the challenge of its competitors by building barriers to defend itself.

These barriers are fine as long as they are *fair*. If a business is well run, or develops a good idea that other businesses can't copy, they deserve to continue to succeed – don't they?

MONOPOLY

ECONOMIES OF SCALE

GOOD IDEAS

MORE EFFICIENT

COMPETITION

Regulating monopolies

In some cases, businesses seek to create *unfair* barriers to their competitors. It's then up to governments to **regulate** the market and ensure competitors have a chance to compete. Regulations known as **competition laws** make unfair barriers illegal.

In 1982, US telephone business AT&T, which owned all the telephone lines in the USA, was deemed to be an unfair monopoly by the government. It was forced to split into seven smaller companies, known as the *Baby Bells*, who had to compete with each other.

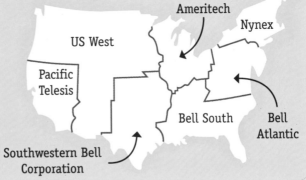

Ameritech

Nynex

US West

Pacific Telesis

Bell South

Bell Atlantic

Southwestern Bell Corporation

Oligopolies

Often markets are controlled not just by one, but a few large businesses. This is known as an **oligopoly.** Here's a (pretend) example:

Checkmates and *Knight's Move* are the two biggest chess-set manufacturers in a country. They don't have many competitors, so they mostly worry about competition from each other.

One business might want to undercut the other one.

At Checkmates, we have decided to lower our prices.

We'll get more customers.

$40 $25 $40

...and more profit.

But they know that the other business is likely to retaliate:

Oh no you don't! BRRRRR!

We'll cut *our* prices too, so we can keep our customers!

$40 $25 $40 $25

Even though we will *both* lose money!

So what's the best thing for these businesses to do?

The branch of economics that models the way rivals interact is known as **game theory** (for more, see page 107). One of the methods game theory uses is mapping out the consequences of different decisions on a grid, like this one:

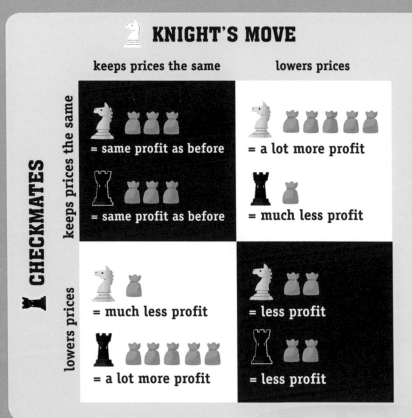

The model predicts that each business will make more profit if it lowers its prices. So *both* firms will end up lowering their prices and making *less* profit – unless they can somehow agree to keep prices high...

Let's agree not to lower our prices. It's bad for our customers...

...but *we'll* both make more profit! We agree!

Big businesses sometimes make an agreement not to compete with each other in order to keep profits high. This is known as a forming a **cartel**. In many countries it is illegal.

How businesses affect the world

Markets are meant to help businesses and consumers agree on a fair price, but sometimes they fail to take everything into account. This kind of market failure is called an **externality**. Here are two examples.

Bee story

A beekeeper produces honey to sell. As well as making honey, her bees fertilize the farms all around her hives. This is a **positive externality**.

Honey $5.00
NOW $2.50

Local farmers grow extra crops, so they make more profit. But the beekeeper finds she can't get a good price for her honey... and in time her business fails, affecting everyone.

The problem is, the market price is only about the honey in each jar. It doesn't reflect the fact that the bees are doing useful work for the local farmers.

Who should pay the true cost of the honey?

Banana story

A banana plantation uses big quantities of chemical fertilizer. Huge numbers of bananas are produced cheaply...

...but when it rains, the fertilizer runs off into local streams. Now river weeds grow so fast they consume all the oxygen in the water.

Without oxygen, many fish die and the local fishing industry begins to struggle. This pollution is a **negative externality**.

Who should pay the fishermen for the loss of their business?

Shouldn't we sort out the pollution problem, too?!

Changing incentives

When externalities cause market failure, it's often up to a government to try to fix things. Spending money is one solution, but the real goal is to change the way businesses – and people – behave.

Positive incentive

To help beekeepers, governments in some countries pay them a regular sum of money known as a **subsidy.** It might seem unfair on other businesses, but it's one way to make sure there are enough beekeepers around to help farmers grow healthy crops.

I'm still not making a profit on the honey...

...but at least I can afford to keep my business going.

Maybe we need to stop using so much fertilizer?

FINE

Negative incentive

Many governments force businesses to pay fines if they are damaging the environment. As long as the fine is big enough to eat into a producer's profits, it forces them to find ways to run their business without creating problems for the world around them.

Governments use incentives to influence the way consumers behave, too. Often they are trying to fix many externalities at once:

The News

AIR QUALITY CRISIS!!
Government offers money to bicycle commuters

OBESITY CRISIS

Positive incentive

By paying a subsidy to commuters to ride bikes to work instead of driving, a government improves air quality and public health.

Negative incentive

By charging commuters for taking their cars into the city, a government reduces air pollution and encourages them to walk or ride a bike.

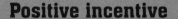

65

Chapter 5:
Economic systems

An **economic system** is a set of rules about how resources get shared out and exchanged.

In some communities, traditions and family ties determine how a harvest is shared out, or how things are made. But in most places, markets and governments have largely taken on these roles.

Governments also collect money from people and businesses, known as **taxes**. Then they decide how to spend that money so it's shared out across society. Deciding how many taxes to collect, and how to spend the money, is a key part of an economic system.

How to share?

In your life, you probably come across different ways of deciding what to do with resources and how to share them out. They are examples of **economic systems** – even though people don't usually call them that.

One person might decide.

You might get to choose.

A group you're part of might decide together.

Or at times, it might feel as if there's no system in place at all.

Sharing goals

Just as at home or school, each country faces the challenge of how to share out resources. Here are some different goals a government might aim for when sharing things out.

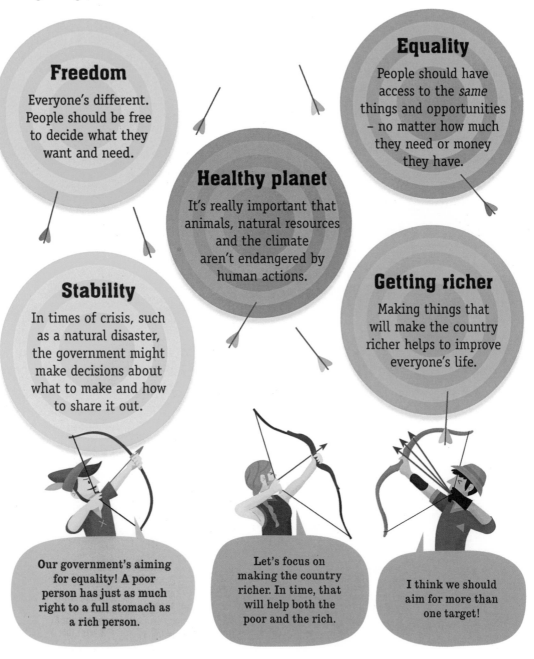

Freedom

Everyone's different. People should be free to decide what they want and need.

Equality

People should have access to the *same* things and opportunities – no matter how much they need or money they have.

Healthy planet

It's really important that animals, natural resources and the climate aren't endangered by human actions.

Stability

In times of crisis, such as a natural disaster, the government might make decisions about what to make and how to share it out.

Getting richer

Making things that will make the country richer helps to improve everyone's life.

Our government's aiming for equality! A poor person has just as much right to a full stomach as a rich person.

Let's focus on making the country richer. In time, that will help both the poor and the rich.

I think we should aim for more than one target!

There's lots of debate about the best way of sharing out resources and running the economy. The next few pages will explore some examples of systems people have tried.

Markets in charge

One way for a government to run an economy is *not* to get involved at all. This is known as a **market economy**, and it was the system in place in Britain for part of the 19th century.

At the time, Britain was undergoing a big change, known as the **Industrial Revolution**.

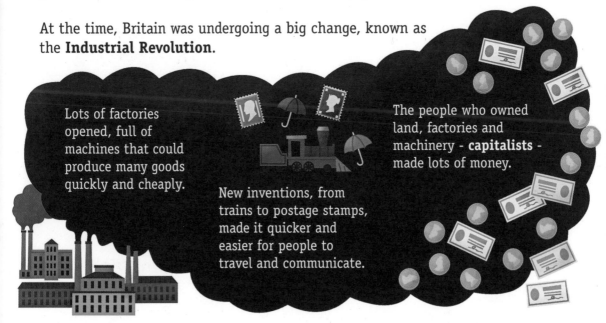

Lots of factories opened, full of machines that could produce many goods quickly and cheaply.

New inventions, from trains to postage stamps, made it quicker and easier for people to travel and communicate.

The people who owned land, factories and machinery - **capitalists** - made lots of money.

The industrial revolution brought prosperity for some, but by the beginning of the 20th century, a quarter of the country was living in poverty. The government's policy was described as *laissez-faire* – which meant "leaving capitalists alone to run their businesses as they like." The system was later named **capitalism**.

What should we do about these problems?

The Old Newsletter
The Old Newsletter

CHILD SLAVES IN FACTORIES

Nothing! If we help the poor, they'll never learn to look after themselves!

DISEASE SPREADS IN CITY SLUMS

OLD TRIBUNE

POTATO CROP FAILURE IN IRELAND KILLS A MILLION

The government's decision not to help didn't resolve problems – if anything they got worse. It became clear that the system needed reform.

Government in charge

To try to fix capitalism, people around the world experimented with giving governments more power. One of the places that made the most drastic changes was Cuba in the 1960s.

A group of revolutionaries overthrew the Cuban government. They set up a system known as **communism**, with the goal of sharing the country's resources equally between Cubans.

They were inspired by the ideas of the German economist Karl Marx.

From each according to his ability, to each according to his need.

Education for all!

Nobody will be jobless or hungry again.

The new government created lots of economic plans – including one to manage food production. This is known as a **planned economy**.

For everyone to have enough to eat, the farmers need to produce....

Cuban Food production (tons)

1,000 t. rice
1,500 t. beans
2,000 t. potatoes

The government also took over all the land, factories and businesses, which helped put the plan into action.

Yessir!

Although resources were mostly shared fairly, there were huge problems too...

It was hard to motivate people to work for the common good...

Why are we producing less food than we used to?

What's the point of me doing all the work if you're just going to take it all!

...and even harder to plan for all the things millions of people might want or need.

LOW STOCK

In practice, giving full control to governments *or* markets hasn't worked. Most countries have since tried to find a more balanced system.

Mixed economies

Nowadays, most countries around the world have some kind of **mixed economy** – where the government is responsible for some things, and the market for others. Here's *roughly* how it works.

Government

The government makes laws that guarantee people's *right* to own things, ideas and designs. It also sets rules about what businesses can and can't do.

The government also tries to manage the economy and set targets about things such as prices, unemployment and poverty.

No child
poverty by
2025

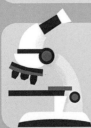

It helps develop future businesses and industries by funding scientific research.

Markets

People have the right to own things, such as...

land

materials

ideas

businesses

machines

...and have the right to exchange them in markets, according to the laws of supply and demand.

The government also produces certain things that benefit all of society and are mostly paid for by taxes. These can include **infrastructure projects** such as building roads, and **public services**, such as waste collection, libraries and education.

What kind of government?

In practice, mixed economies vary country by country, depending on whether the government that's in power is "big" or "small." This describes how much control a government takes over its economy, businesses and even individuals.

BIG government often means **MORE...**

Small government often means **LESS...**

...money spent on public services

...regulation of businesses

...laws about what people can and can't do

...taxes

How a government acts also depends on its beliefs about the best way to organize a society. The words **left-wing** and **right-wing** are sometimes used to describe these beliefs.

Common left-wing ideas

People and businesses, especially rich ones, should give back to society by paying high taxes.

Some businesses, such as water companies, should be state-owned because they're for everyone.

The government should protect and pay for the weakest and most vulnerable people.

Common right-wing ideas

Individuals and businesses are better at running their own lives than the government is.

It's the government's job to keep people safe, not to tell them what to do.

Lower taxes encourage people to make more money. This makes the whole country better off.

Most people *and* governments support a mixture of left-wing and right-wing ideas, and prefer a big government approach for some issues, but not others.

Left out

Governments often have to try to please different groups, who want or need different things, with a limited amount of money. Usually, they end up helping some groups, while others get left out – whether that's families, pensioners, students, people out of work or refugees like this family...

We left our country because living there was dangerous. This new country says it will keep us safe, but we can't yet apply for a job...

...or go to school.

No country's economic system is perfect. You'll find some ideas for improving them in chapters 6 and 8.

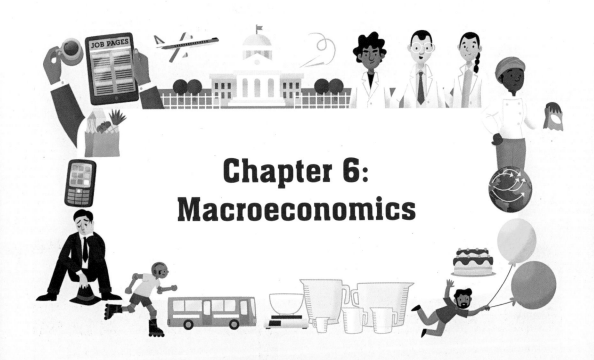

Chapter 6:
Macroeconomics

Macroeconomics is about looking at the BIG
picture – the economy as a whole.
Are people getting richer or poorer?
Are more businesses opening or closing?
Are things getting more expensive or cheaper?
And what can governments do?

The choices governments make about what to
do (or not to do), are known as **policies**.
When people vote on a new government,
one big question they ask is, "Would their
policies be successful?"

Big picture

In economics, you can look at a problem from the point of view of a person or business. For example, "Why is it hard to find a job?"

Or, you can zoom out and look at what's going on in the whole economy. For example, "Why are LOTS of people finding it hard to find a job?"

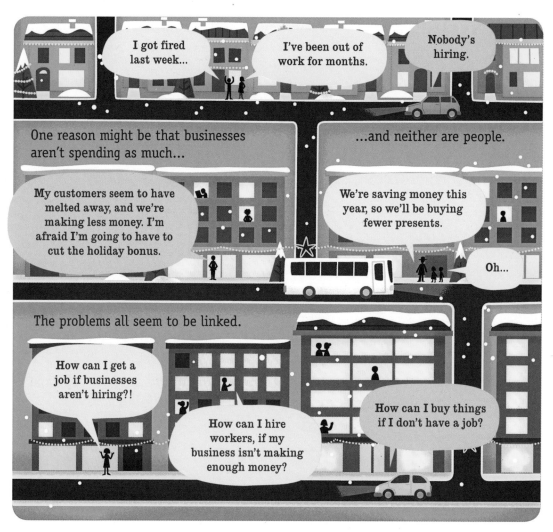

How are problems in an economy linked? What's caused them? What might fix or prevent them? These BIG QUESTIONS are what macroeconomics is all about.

Big choices

When it comes to issues that affect the economy of a whole country, there's not much one person or business can do. Generally it's up to governments to try to manage the economy to make sure it's working as well as possible. What the government does is a bit like what this baker does...

The baker has a vision of the perfect cake.

Each government has an idea of what the perfect economy looks like.
For example, plentiful well-paid jobs, top-quality schools and hospitals, a clean, healthy environment...

There are lots of different recipes the baker can try in the quest for the perfect cake.

COOK BOOKS

There are so many!

Which one should I try?

Government officials can try all sorts of different ideas and policies suggested by economists.

Making the cake then requires careful measurement. So does managing an economy, except instead of flour, you measure things like unemployment.

Growth

Unemployment

Prices

However grand the vision, bakers and governments are limited by the ingredients they've got and the environment they're working in.

Mmm, I've run out of money for more flour.

Sometimes things go mostly to plan, and sometimes they really don't...

Of course the economy *isn't* a cake, and managing it is a big responsibility. The decisions people in power make have huge consequences on people's lives – much more than a burned cake.

Measuring the economy

Government economists measure as much of the economy as they can, to spot patterns and problems that might need fixing. An important measure is the value of everything produced in a country over a period of time. This is known as **Gross Domestic Product** (**GDP**).

One way to work out GDP is to add up how much has been spent on everything that's been produced in a country in a year. For example, the GDP of the US in 2018 was made up of...

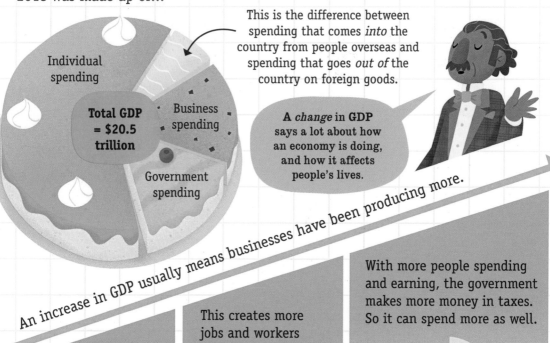

Individual spending

Total GDP = $20.5 trillion

Business spending

Government spending

This is the difference between spending that comes *into* the country from people overseas and spending that goes *out of* the country on foreign goods.

A *change* in GDP says a lot about how an economy is doing, and how it affects people's lives.

An increase in GDP usually means businesses have been producing more.

Businesses are making more money, so they tend to spend more.

We're going to spend $1 million developing a new cancer treatment.

This creates more jobs and workers feel more confident about the future.

I've just got a steady job in a lab. I've spent my first pay check on rollerblades!

With more people spending and earning, the government makes more money in taxes. So it can spend more as well.

New university science wing

More production and spending can create a positive cycle where people are generally better off. If GDP increases for more than six months, the economy is said to be **growing**.

Not the only goal

Governments often set themselves the goal of increasing GDP, with the hope that it will make people better off and improve their quality of life. But GDP only measures things that have a price, so focusing on it can lead to forgetting LOTS of other really important things, such as...

Free work

GDP doesn't take into account all the work parents and caregivers do at home for free, such as teaching kids to read, or doing housework.

Environment

Nature does a lot of essential work for free, too. For example, forests clean the air we breathe, but they only become valuable in GDP terms if they're sold and chopped down.

Inequality

A rich country with high GDP can still have lots of poor people, if the riches aren't shared out fairly.

> We need to make sure that increases in **GDP** don't come at the expense of the planet.

A decrease in GDP usually means businesses have been producing less.

Businesses are making less money. There's less to do, so fewer people are hired.

> We've sold so little this year, I can't afford to keep employing you.

The future looks uncertain, so people spend less.

> We should probably save money in case we lose our jobs, too.

The government has less money because people are paying lower taxes.

> We can't afford to pay university fees for all students.

> Maybe we could borrow some money?

A fall in production and spending can create a negative cycle, where people are generally worse off. If GDP falls for more than six months, the economy is said to be in a **recession**. Most economies follow a pattern of good times followed by bad ones.

More measurements

As well as GDP, economists measure all sorts of other things to get an idea of how the economy is affecting people's lives. These are known as **economic indicators**.

Are things getting more expensive, or less?

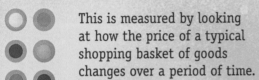

This is measured by looking at how the price of a typical shopping basket of goods changes over a period of time.

Last year $50

This year $51

Prices almost always increase over time. This is known as **inflation**. People don't tend to notice if prices creep up slowly, but they do if things get more expensive quickly.

If prices are decreasing, it's known as **deflation**. It sounds great, but it often means people stop spending – nobody wants to spend money *now* on something that will be cheaper tomorrow.

How many people are out of work?

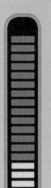

The number of people who want a job but don't have one is known as **unemployment**.

Governments generally want to keep unemployment low, but there will always be some people without jobs.

How much are people earning?

This is measured by monitoring weekly average wages, which tend to increase a bit every year.

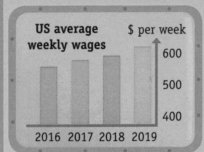

US average weekly wages $ per week

600

500

400

2016 2017 2018 2019

Wages are often compared with inflation. If *wages* don't increase as quickly as *prices*, people will end up poorer.

I've finished the unemployment report!

Great! Now start again.

ALL these numbers are constantly changing, so the official figures only ever show a moment in time.

What can governments do?

Governments can use certain tools, such as **taxes**, to try to manage the economy. It's up to a government to decide what to tax and how much to collect.

In most countries today, individuals and businesses pay taxes on what they *earn* – whether that's wages or profits.

They may also pay taxes on what they *own,* such as property, and what they *buy* (the price of most things you buy includes a sales tax).

I'm paid $40,000 per year to do this job. I have to pay $4,300 in taxes.

This shop makes about $25,000 profit a year. I have to pay $5,000 of that in taxes.

I'm paying $10 for the box of chocolates – of which $1 is tax.

Governments use taxes to try to make the economy...

...greener, safer, healthier.

Taxes can be used to increase the price of things that might be damaging to society, and discourage buyers.

...bigger.

Cutting taxes, for example for businesses, means they have more money to spend, make and hire. Helping businesses can make the economy grow.

...fairer.

Most governments charge higher earners higher taxes, to pay for things that mostly help poor people (see more on the next page).

Finding the right BALANCE with taxes is tricky.

TOO MUCH and people will try to find ways of not paying it – such as moving to another country.

TOO LITTLE and there won't be enough money to pay for things such as new roads or better schools.

Government spending

A major job of government is to choose how to spend its money.
These are some of the things they can spend it on.

Social protection

Supporting people struggling due to unemployment, disability, old age or all sorts of other reasons.

Public services

Services everybody needs such as education, healthcare, policing.

Infrastructure

Building and maintaining things such as roads, bridges and internet cables.

Governments can use spending as a tool to make the economy...

...greener.

The government can spend money on things that do not cause pollution, such as wind turbines.

...fairer.

Spending money on things that give all people better opportunities and good quality public services, whether they are rich or poor.

...more productive.

For example, by spending money to improve internet speeds.

Government borrowing

Governments often want to spend more money than they can collect in taxes, so they increase their funds by *borrowing* money, often from a bank or another country. But a government can only afford to borrow so much, because they have to pay that money back, including extra money, known as **interest**.

In 2018, the US Government spent **$4.1 trillion**...

...of which **$390 billion** was spent paying back interest it owed.

Can't the government just print **MORE** money?

We can print a little, but too much and the money becomes worthless.

All governments borrow money and over time this can get *really* expensive.
So governments have to find a balance between spending, printing and borrowing.

Interest rates

It's not just governments that borrow money; businesses and individuals borrow too. Another tool the government can use to steer the economy is to change **interest rates** – the amount banks charge for borrowing money.

The government works with a national bank, often known as the central bank, to do this.

Increasing interest rates makes it more expensive to borrow money, while decreasing them makes it cheaper.

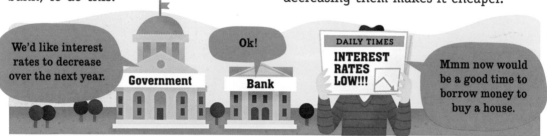

We'd like interest rates to decrease over the next year.

Government

Ok!

Bank

DAILY TIMES
INTEREST RATES LOW!!!

Mmm now would be a good time to borrow money to buy a house.

Lowering interest rates can help to boost the economy by encouraging people and businesses to borrow more, and then to spend more.

In practice

Nobody knows exactly what will happen when a government uses any of these tools, because there are so many other factors to think about. For example, here's why cutting interest rates might not have the effect a government expects.

In theory...

Let's cut interest rates. People will borrow, spend and produce more, so the economy will grow!

HIGH

Interest rates

LOW

In reality...

My business is in lots of debt already, so I'm in no rush to borrow more.

We're barely out of a recession. I'll wait and see before I borrow money to buy a house.

The cost of my groceries has gone up, so I'm having to cut back, not borrow to spend *more*.

So people in government have to make their best guess at what will work. Even with the best intentions, they can't seem to stop economic crises from occurring every decade or so.

Crisis!

Economists study past recessions in order to try to avoid repeating mistakes in the future. One of the worst, the Great Depression, started in the USA and spread all around the world.

Oct 1929

The stock market crashed.

I invested all my savings to buy company stocks.

The stocks are now worth nothing.

I've lost everything.

Jan 1930

The rest of the US economy wasn't doing well either.

A drought has destroyed all my crops.

Nobody's buying cars. I've fired 75,000 workers.

Jan 1931

Millions wandered the roads looking for work.

Jan 1932

The crisis spread to all the countries that depended on trade with America.

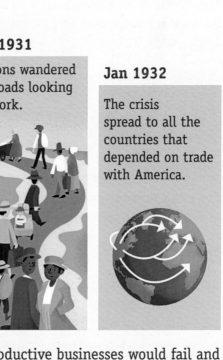

Most economists at the time thought that unproductive businesses would fail and the rest would start rehiring and the economy would recover. But for years, it didn't. A British economist, John Maynard Keynes, came up with an explanation.

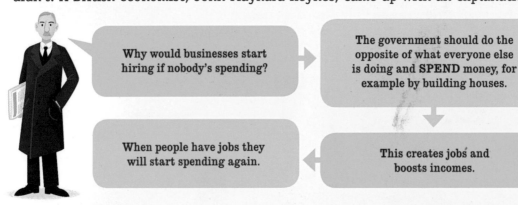

Why would businesses start hiring if nobody's spending?

The government should do the opposite of what everyone else is doing and **SPEND** money, for example by building houses.

When people have jobs they will start spending again.

This creates jobs and boosts incomes.

For over a decade after the depression, US President Roosevelt did just that, spending huge sums on building projects and creating jobs. But he also printed lots of money, reduced interest rates and raised taxes – so it's hard to know exactly what caused the economy to recover.

During the Great Depression a fall in *demand* was one of the triggers of the crisis. But sometimes, a crisis is triggered by a fall in *supply*.

In 1973, oil-producing Arab countries stopped selling oil to the US and other countries.

This was in protest at the US and its allies supporting Israel in a war between Israel and a group of Arab countries.

CLOSED FOR BUSINESS

The price of oil rocketed. So did the price of things transported or made using oil – which was *everything*.

Rising prices (inflation) combined with a period of high unemployment led to a recession. Economists were confused about how to solve these two problems.

To bring prices down, we need people to spend **LESS**.

So increase taxes!

Increase interest rates!

Lower government spending!

But to get businesses hiring again, we need people to spend **MORE**.

So lower taxes!

Lower interest rates!

Increase government spending!

Some governments tried to reduce inflation by increasing interest rates.

If you want to borrow money it's going to cost you a **LOT**.

GREEN TREE BANK

20% INTEREST

Mmm, no thanks.

People stopped spending, and prices started to decrease again, but a series of recessions was triggered.

MARCH FOR JOBS

Was it worth it? We all really suffered.

As recessions throughout the 20th century showed, there is no neat and easy solution for solving crises. Governments and economists often end up having to choose between two bad options.

People at work

Most people around the world spend more time at work than they do with their families. It's work that turns seeds into food, wood into paper and ideas into inventions. Work is a huge market, and here's how the market for work *works*.

The rules of work

To protect workers, governments set and enforce rules that make working fairer and safer. These are known as **workers' rights**, and they include the right...

...to fair pay.

...to be safe and healthy at work.

...to paid time off.

...to a childhood. (Most countries set laws that mean children can't do paid work.)

Some rules increase the cost of work.

So governments have to consider the costs and benefits of each rule.

Unemployment

According to the laws of supply and demand, in theory people would only ever be out of work temporarily. In THEORY...

| If the demand for work drops... | → | ...people lose their jobs. | → | So workers are willing to work for less. | → | Wages fall, making it cheaper to hire. | → | Employers are able to hire again. |

But, in REALITY, in most countries there are always people out of work, sometimes quite a few and some for a long time.

People don't always live in the places where businesses are looking for workers.

When businesses are struggling, managers find it's easier to simply fire *some* workers, rather than cut wages for *all* workers.

Unemployment depends on how the rest of the economy is doing.

There's often a mismatch between the skills workers have and the skills businesses need.

There's a recession on! Even if wages are low, I won't take the risk of hiring people until the economy gets better.

I lost my job as a coal miner. Nobody else wants my coal-mining skills.

Being out of work is really tough financially, and it often affects people's mental and physical health badly, too. So it's one of the big challenges governments tackle. Here are some of the things that can help.

Boost the economy. If the economy is doing well, businesses will hire more.

Spend money helping workers to retrain to get skills that employers need.

Make it cheaper to hire workers, for example by reducing taxes companies have to pay.

Create incentives for businesses to hire people who find it harder to get a job – such as young people with no experience.

Poverty

Most people agree that everyone should have the chance to have a decent life. Yet in reality, some people have so little that they struggle day-to-day. Measuring poverty is the first step to making sure the economy is working for everybody, not just the rich.

Who is poor?

Look at these families living in India, the UK and the USA...

We survive on subsidized rice from the government and any fish we can catch.

Income per week:
448 rupees ($6.50)

We've got to choose between spending money on food or spending it on heating.

Income per week:
£340 ($420)

I've lost my job. Hopefully I'll get a new one soon. In the meantime we have savings to get by, and we own a house, so we don't pay rent.

Income per week:
$0

What these families show is that poverty isn't just a number. The family in the middle earns more than 60 times the family on the left, but they're both unable to meet their basic needs. The family on the right has no income, but has earned lots in the past, and probably will in the future, too.

One definition of **poverty** is not having enough money to take part in the society you live in. In a study carried out in the UK, people said this meant not having enough money for essentials such as...

...food

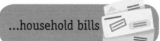
...household bills

...clothes

...transportation

But it also included things such as...

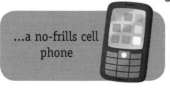
...a no-frills cell phone

...being able to give a present

...having a meal out a couple of times a year

By this measure, in the UK, just over 1 person in 5 is living in poverty.

Poverty trap

Making the most of your talent and creating a secure life takes that much more skill, willpower and luck if you're poor. On the flip side, once you're rich it's easier to stay rich. Here's the difference being born rich or poor can make...

If you're poor it's harder to get a good education...

...so jobs tend to be lower-paid and more uncertain...

...and bad luck has bigger consequences.

Born poor

Mom, can you help with my homework?

Sorry, I'm going to my evening job.

This was the best job I could get. It's low-paid, and I'll never get promoted.

I've injured my leg so I had to stop work. I've not found a new job yet.

STILL POOR

Born rich

Mom, can you help with my homework?

I've called a tutor to help you.

I've just started at a well-paid job – with great chances of promotion!

The company will pay for you to take a taxi to work until you recover.

STILL RICH

Poverty is a huge waste of potential and deeply unfair. Left unchecked, the gap between rich and poor, known as **inequality**, tends to increase.

Here are some popular policy ideas that some people believe can help. It's not just about sharing around, but changing the conditions that keep people poor.

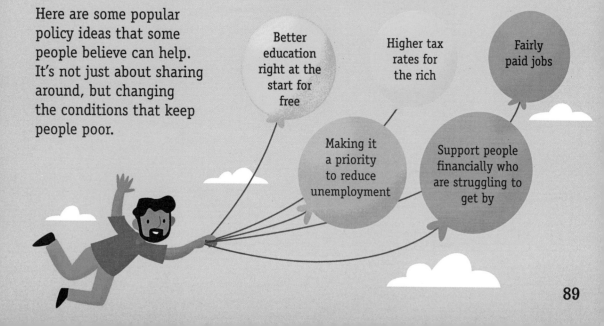

Better education right at the start for free

Higher tax rates for the rich

Fairly paid jobs

Making it a priority to reduce unemployment

Support people financially who are struggling to get by

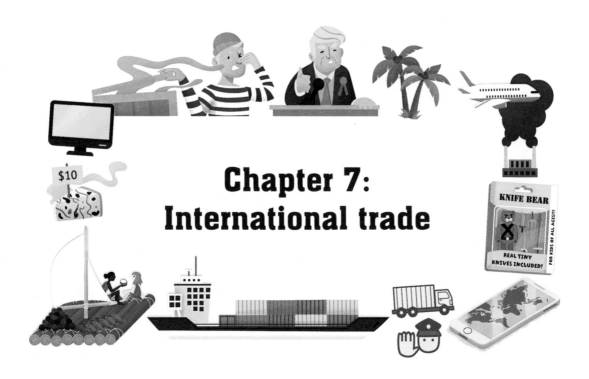

Chapter 7:
International trade

For thousands of years, ships have crossed stormy seas, caravans have tramped across endless deserts and ox-carts have trundled down pot-holed roads. All that enormous effort was worth it so that people could trade, not just locally, but with people from around the world.

Trade gives people greater choice, lowers prices and brings essential resources to places where they might not be available. Trading over long distances makes markets more efficient and increases competition. But, despite all those benefits, the very idea of trading across borders can be controversial.

Imports and exports

Some countries produce certain goods more cheaply than other countries. **Trade** means exchanging these cheap goods for other countries' cheap goods.

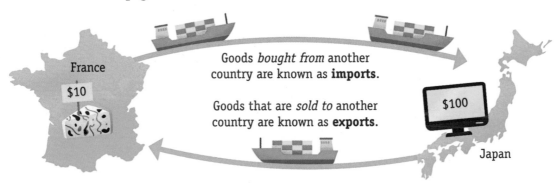

France

$10

Goods *bought from* another country are known as **imports**.

Goods that are *sold to* another country are known as **exports**.

$100

Japan

For example, France makes blue cheese more cheaply than Japan. Japan produces TVs more cheaply than France. It makes sense for French cheesemongers to make extra cheese to export, and for Japanese engineers to make and export extra TVs. Consumers in both countries will end up with better things, and cheaper, too.

Long distance trade is not easy. There are many logistical barriers that make it harder and more expensive to move large amounts of goods across borders (for example, cheese).

Urk! That stinks!

CHEESE

Other barriers are intentionally put up by countries to make trade more difficult, such as charging a border tax, or **tariff**.

Tariffs protect local businesses by making it more expensive for foreign businesses to compete with them.

We want to sell our high-quality Danish combs in America.

You'll have to pay us a $5 tariff for each comb first.

COMB

HOME HQ

USA CUSTOMS OFFICE

I'd love to try a Danish comb, but they're so expensive!

DANISH COMBS $6.99

USA COMBS $1.99

Tariffs or free trade?

Politicians are often tempted to use tariffs. Tariffs make it harder for foreign businesses to sell their goods, which pleases local businesses and wins votes.

Vote for me and big tariffs! I vow to make Americans buy American products again.

YEAH! We want to keep our jobs.

Tariffs will keep my comb factory open. I'm voting for him!

Protecting AMERICAN jobs

Although this might seem a good idea, there are problems with tariffs. Many economists believe that governments should do everything they can to remove them, and promote a low-tariffs policy, generally known as **free trade**.

Free trade brings more competition, which makes everything cheaper.

And if we don't have to make everything ourselves, we can specialize in what we do best.

Tariffs makes products more expensive for local consumers.

And less competition means the protected businesses get away with being less efficient.

Vote for me, and I'll sign as many free trade agreements as I can. More trade will make all of us richer!

But what about my job? I'm not voting for you.

We will support you financially if you lose your job and help you retrain.

FREE TRADE FOR ALL

Since 1945, free trade economists have been winning the argument. Despite the controversy, many countries have dropped most tariffs and become more open and more linked together – although all countries still keep some barriers to trade. This is part of a process known as **globalization.**

Why free trade works – in theory

Many economists believe free trade benefits everyone because of an elegant economic theory called **comparative advantage**, invented two hundred years ago. Here's how it works...

Imagine that Liz and Carrie have been shipwrecked on a desert island. They have two main tasks: collecting coconuts and catching fish to survive.

Carrie is very good at these jobs. She can catch 20 fish a day *or* collect 20 coconuts a day.

Liz isn't so good at either job. She can catch 2 fish *or* 18 coconuts a day.

Carrie is better at producing both coconuts *and* fish. So is it actually worth her sharing the workload and the food with Liz if she is simply better at doing everything? The surprising answer is **YES**, because of what it *costs* her to do the work.

Whenever Carrie spends time collecting 1 fish it costs her the time she could have spent collecting 1 coconut.

Whenever Carrie spends time collecting 1 coconut it costs her 1 fish.

Whenever Liz spends time catching 1 fish it costs her the time she could have spent collecting 9 coconuts. That's **expensive**.

Whenever Liz spends time collecting 1 coconut it costs her 1/9 of a fish. That's **cheap**.

It costs me less than Liz to collect fish – so I'll do the fishing.

It costs me much, much less to collect coconuts than Carrie – so I'll climb palm trees!

Although Carrie is a little faster at collecting coconuts, Liz has a much lower opportunity cost when she collects them. This is called a **comparative advantage**. It means the best way to collect food on the desert island is for each of the castaways to *specialize* in producing whatever leads them to give up the least and then trade for what they don't have.

This is how much food is produced after 10 days if they *don't* specialize and trade.

This is how much food is produced after 10 days when they *do* specialize and trade.

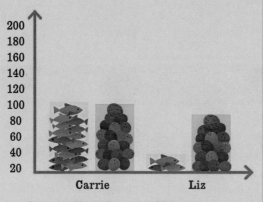

After 10 days they would have 110 fish and 190 coconuts.

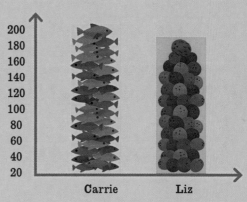

After 10 days they would have 200 fish and 180 coconuts.

Hope you like coconut milk.

Comparative advantage works on desert islands and it works in the real world as well. If every country is free to produce what they make most efficiently and trade for what they can't produce so efficiently, more things get made overall, of better quality, and cheaper.

But this is only possible if countries trade freely with each other. In theory, free trade makes life cheaper and better for *everyone*.

Reasons for barriers

All governments want *some* control over what is sold in their country, so they often still keep some tariffs and trade barriers.

It can be very hard for a new business to compete with well-established ones. Here's an example from 60 years ago...

I want to set up a steel mill here in South Korea. But international companies make steel better and cheaper so we can't compete.

Let's put a temporary tariff on foreign steel, then at least we can sell our own steel here.

South Korea

For fifty years, the South Korean government protected many infant companies with tariffs. Today, these have become world-class competitors.

Some industries could be dangerous if they were controlled by another country.

Sorry, you can't set up a nuclear power plant in our country. We don't trust you!

We're not selling you our super-laser! You might fire it at our soldiers.

Most governments – and people – agree that there are certain things no one should manufacture or sell. At least, not to just anyone. Many governments demand that products do not harm the environment, are safe for children, and have safety warnings on them. These are known as **non-tariff barriers**.

KNIFE BEAR

FOR KIDS OF ALL AGES!!!

REAL TINY KNIVES INCLUDED!

INGREDIENTS: TOO MUCH SUGAR SALT FAT

Any barrier to trade can lead to anger between countries. They often accuse each other of lying about why a barrier has been put in place – and that can lead to trade wars...

Trade wars are risky

If a government sets high tariffs, other countries are likely to respond by bringing in tariffs of their own. Your tariffs might stop imports from coming in, but they will stop your exports from leaving, too.

If rival countries bring in higher and higher tariffs, it's a form of conflict called a **trade war**. Trade wars are difficult to win, because everyone suffers. A famous example occurred during the Great Depression.

In 1930, American farmers and manufacturers were struggling. To help them, the government quadrupled tariffs on 900 imported items.

The tariffs worked. American imports of foreign goods plunged 66%.

But other countries retaliated with tariffs of their own. American exports plunged by 61%.

International trade ground to a halt. By 1934, American GDP had halved and world trade had shrunk by 66%. Thousands of firms went out of business, and millions more people became unemployed. It was a global disaster.

Trading blocs

Sometimes, groups of countries sign free-trade agreements with each other, forming **trading blocs**. Examples include the EU in Europe, or MERCOSUR in South America. All members agree to trade freely with each other. Sometimes, blocs also agree to put up joint tariff and non-tariff barriers to make trade with non-members *more* expensive.

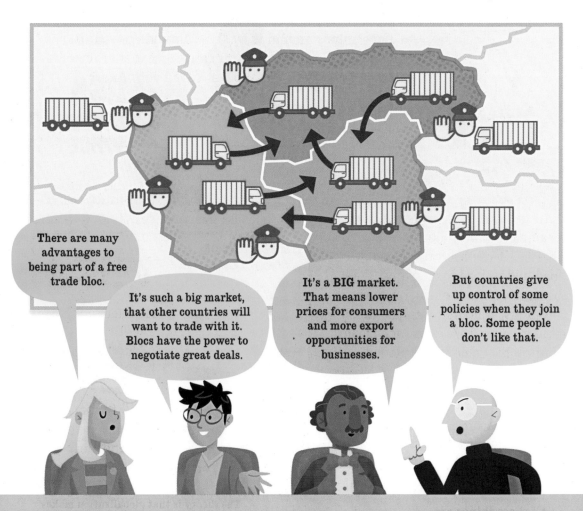

There are many advantages to being part of a free trade bloc.

It's such a big market, that other countries will want to trade with it. Blocs have the power to negotiate great deals.

It's a **BIG** market. That means lower prices for consumers and more export opportunities for businesses.

But countries give up control of some policies when they join a bloc. Some people don't like that.

Some trading blocs are simply to do with trading goods and services. Others, such as the EU, allow people and money to move around freely as well. People can live and work in any member country, and be paid and pay taxes where they live.

Sometimes a country may believe that another country or bloc has acted unfairly. If this happens they can appeal to the **World Trade Organization** (WTO), an international organization that provides rules for settling trade disputes and negotiating new agreements.

Globalization

Globalization is a way of describing a huge economy that includes practically the whole world. In recent years this global economy has grown enormously, partly because of free trade, but also for two other simple reasons: **containerization** and **communication**.

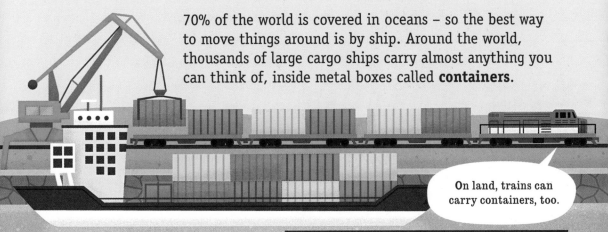

70% of the world is covered in oceans – so the best way to move things around is by ship. Around the world, thousands of large cargo ships carry almost anything you can think of, inside metal boxes called **containers**.

On land, trains can carry containers, too.

In 1945 it used to take a week to load and unload cargo ships. Now, because of the container system, it takes just 6 hours to unload much bigger ships. This efficiency means that global trade has exploded in the last 70 years.

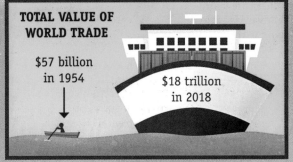

TOTAL VALUE OF WORLD TRADE

$57 billion in 1954

$18 trillion in 2018

With the invention of the internet and email, it takes no time at all for people on the other side of the world to talk. Running a global business is easier than ever, and large businesses can coordinate production across many countries.

Your international phone!

All these things are in a smartphone...

Gyroscope from Switzerland

Camera from Japan

Battery from China

Glass screen from USA

Gold from Ghana

The theory is that globalization makes economies more efficient, and helps people everywhere to get richer, and have better, cheaper choices. But has this really worked? Turn the page to find out.

99

Globalization – winners and losers

WINNER: lots of people

Although the world's population has grown enormously, the number of people living in extreme poverty has actually gone *down*.

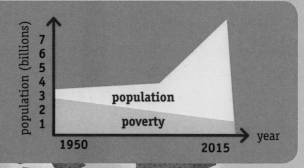

Can we make rules to make shipping greener?

LOSER: independence

International trade rules and agreements often restrict what policies or laws a country can use. Other countries will stop trading with countries that break the rules.

WINNER: technology

Trade allows countries to specialize in what they do best, because they no longer have to produce everything they need. Over the past fifty years this focus has been a big factor in the world's rapid technological development.

In a more connected world, good ideas and innovations spread much faster. After gunpowder was invented by the Chinese, it took 300 years to reach Europe. This would not be the case today.

LOSER: accountability

Because the world's biggest companies operate in many countries, it is sometimes hard for individual countries to make them follow rules or pay a fair amount of taxes.

WINNER: development

Globalization has brought new jobs and opportunities to places such as China, India and Indonesia. Billions of people in these countries have been lifted out of extreme poverty.

LOSER: some workers

Businesses often move factories overseas to countries with cheaper workers. The workers left behind often struggle to find new jobs or retrain. Without help from governments, small towns and even whole regions can find globalization a painful process.

CLOSED

Good idea!

LOSER: carbon emissions

More trade means more production and transportation. This creates more carbon dioxide, which has caused our current climate crisis.

LOSER: small countries

Big trading blocs can get great deals for themselves... ...but this means smaller countries get the bad end of the same deal, so it's hard for their economies to grow.

WINNER: cooperation

For trade to flourish, countries must cooperate with each other. Working together, they can tackle big issues such as migration and climate change.

I'd sign that treaty!

LOSER: *too* specialized

Sometimes countries (especially poorer ones) are forced to specialize in exporting a single commodity such as gold, coffee or bananas. But it is risky to rely on just one export. The country is very vulnerable if prices, or people's tastes change.

What do you own that comes from overseas?

Free trade **HAS** made many people and countries wealthier – but it has caused problems, too.

Chapter 8:
Big questions
(and a few answers)

There is almost no limit to the questions economics can tackle. Economists use their skills to analyze the problems, both big and small, that face the world today.

This chapter explores just a few of these questions, as well as asking what type of answers we should be looking for.

Can economics help save the planet?

When fossil fuels such as oil and coal are used, they give out carbon dioxide, a gas that warms the planet. We have known this for decades, but are still using more and more fossil fuels each year.

We are even finding new ways of getting them out of the ground.

There's a big opportunity here. We can make BILLIONS.

In 2018, United Nations scientists warned that by 2030, if nothing was done, colossally damaging global heating would occur.

But will we be able to change in time?

Change is hard. People, businesses and nations don't like policies that make them poorer in the short-term.

NO MORE FUEL TAXES

Green taxes are making fuel too expensive!

It is tricky to get large groups of people to make sacrifices and work together voluntarily, even if it makes a lot of sense.

It's not fair, the RICH countries – who pollute the most – should cut back more.

We won't cut back unless EVERYONE does.

Markets alone can't make us change, because businesses and people don't suffer the FULL cost of their choices.

Or not YET, at least! People are very bad at thinking about the damage they may be doing to the FUTURE.

But we don't have the time or the opportunity to design a whole new way of doing things.

So we'll have to work with what we've got.

There's no time for despair because there's still time to change. If enough people CHOOSE to change their spending habits, markets and businesses will respond.

Individuals can...

Choose not to fly. Plane travel is the fastest growing source of carbon dioxide pollution.

Eat less meat. Farming animals consumes enormous amounts of resources and land.

Repair things instead of throwing them away. This saves resources.

Choose locally produced goods, even if they are more expensive. This cuts transportation pollution.

But the biggest and most important choices will have to be made by *societies*. Only governments can pass laws or raise taxes to change EVERYONE'S incentives. Here's one idea: bringing in a global tax on the use of fossil fuels.

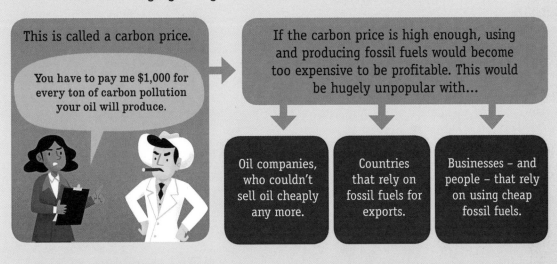

This is called a carbon price.

You have to pay me $1,000 for every ton of carbon pollution your oil will produce.

If the carbon price is high enough, using and producing fossil fuels would become too expensive to be profitable. This would be hugely unpopular with...

Oil companies, who couldn't sell oil cheaply any more.

Countries that rely on fossil fuels for exports.

Businesses – and people – that rely on using cheap fossil fuels.

The people who don't want these changes to happen often make an economic argument. They say "It's too expensive to change, people will lose their jobs." But there's a powerful economic argument for finding alternatives to fossil fuels.

The Stern Review of the economics of climate change estimated that the cost of dealing with climate change now = **2% of global GDP.**

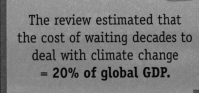

The review estimated that the cost of waiting decades to deal with climate change = **20% of global GDP.**

How do wars start?

Since the time of our earliest ancestors, wars have started for a wide variety of political, historical and even psychological reasons. But most wars have had important *economic* causes too.

Resources

War was an important part of the Roman Empire's economy. Rome benefited greatly from luxury goods, mines and grain-producing regions that it conquered. Today, countries fight to control valuable resources such as oil fields.

International trade

In the 19th century, the British Empire made vast profits selling a highly-addictive drug called opium to China.

When the Chinese Emperor banned the opium trade to protect his people, the British invaded China twice, in 1839 and 1856, in order to keep their drug-pushing operation going.

Scarcity and corruption

One of the causes of the Syrian civil war, which began in 2011, was a major drought. Syria's water-starved farms failed. Farmers fled to cities, but even there, food and jobs were in short supply.

On top of *that*, people were angry with the government for unfairly taking and distributing jobs, food and resources.

In 2011, mass protests began against the government. The government responded with violence and civil war broke out.

How to stop wars

One reason that economists studied **game theory** (see page 63) was as a way of predicting how to win a nuclear war. It turned out that winning involved *not fighting at all.*

Between 1945 and 1991, relations between the USA and the Soviet Union (Russia and other states) were extremely tense, partly because both countries had deadly nuclear weapons.

Here's where game theory came in. A famous game had two sides choosing whether to betray the other or cooperate.

I like betrayal! We should bomb them first, before they bomb us!

The striking lesson from the game was that if you couldn't trust the other player, the most logical outcome was *always* to betray.

So both sides knew the most logical step for their enemy was to start a surprise nuclear war.

End of the world

According to the theory, the only way to prevent an attack was to build *so many* bombs that both nations knew neither side could survive a war.

This was described as a deterrent.

The deterrent took away any incentive to betray the other and helped them to cooperate.

Some economists believe that wars can be stopped by global trade too.

I'd argue that the more a country trades with other countries, the less likely it is to go to war with them.

Right, countries that depend on each other have more to lose from conflict.

Also, stopping trade with another country is a way to send a message without resorting to actual fighting.

That's true, but don't forget that punishing a country by stopping its trade could cause as much devastation as a war.

Why is technology so important?

People often get really excited about new gadgets – some even camp overnight in a store parking lot to be the first to get their hands on a new phone. But *nobody* gets more excited about technology – even the humble electrical washing machine – than an economist.

Since its invention over 100 years ago, the electrical washing machine has...

...saved SO MUCH time, especially for women doing chores at home. This has freed up time for women to get paid work outside the home.

...changed the kinds of jobs women do. In the 1870s in the US, around 50% of working women were employed in domestic services, while under 1% are now.

New machines, ideas and ways of doing things can change the way people live. New technologies also allow people to make more with less, which is how economies grow. Governments can encourage this by...

...providing infrastructure like broadband cables.

...funding research.

...protecting ideas with laws, so people can create new things without worrying they'll be stolen.

What about jobs?

I used to have a job as a housekeeper, but nobody's hiring any more.

I'm sorry mom. *I've* benefitted though...

In most economies, about 10% of jobs are destroyed each year by new technologies and about the same number are created. But when a factory closes in a town, a whole community can become unemployed, and those individuals pay the cost – unless governments support them.

Throughout history, people have worried that eventually technology will wipe out more jobs than can be created – but so far this has not been the case.

Is inequality ok?

Economists aren't the only ones who can answer economic questions. For example, American philosopher John Rawls explored people's feelings about inequality by getting them to imagine an ideal world.

1 In this world, there will be two groups of equal sizes, called "richer" and "poorer."

2 YOU will get to live in this world, *after* you've answered the question – "how rich should each group be?"

3 Then, a flip of a coin will determine which group you go in.

In lots of countries, people taking part in the exercise tend to design a world with inequality, where the rich earn a bit more than the poor – but not too much more. Here are some of their reasons.

It's only *fair* if people who work harder or better are rewarded for it.

Yes but, when a company's managers earn hundreds of times more than an unskilled worker, that's *unfair*. There's only so much more a manager can achieve in a day!

Inequality is also *motivating*. Hard work, good ideas and taking risks needs to be rewarded, otherwise people wouldn't bother.

But knowing you're at the bottom can be *demotivating*, especially if you think you'll never do well, however hard you work.

Ok so *some* inequality is good, but not too much.

Interestingly, these imaginary, but still unequal, worlds were much more equal than the *real* world is. And more equal than most people realize, too. A 2017 study in the US showed that people thought the richest 20% of the population...

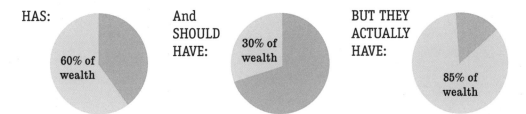

HAS: 60% of wealth

And SHOULD HAVE: 30% of wealth

BUT THEY ACTUALLY HAVE: 85% of wealth

Even if people think *some* inequality is ok, this seems unfair. Do you think everyone in your country has a fair chance to become rich, successful or happy?

Are we running out of resources?

The Earth can only replace some of the resources we use each year. A group of researchers called the Global Footprint Network calculate the day each year we start using resources that won't be replaced.

In 2019, it fell on July 29th, the earliest day yet. It means that right now we are using up the Earth's resources 1.75 times faster than they can be replaced.

The group calculates how much we use by looking at *everything* we consume. They include resources such as the forests' capacity to suck up carbon dioxide. They also calculate how many Earths we'd need if *everyone* had the same lifestyle as people in some of the richest countries in 2019.

United States	5.0 Earths
Australia	4.1 Earths
Russia	3.2 Earths
Japan	2.8 Earths
United Kingdom	2.7 Earths
China	2.2 Earths
Brazil	1.7 Earths
India	0.7 Earths
World Average	1.75 Earths

It is unlikely that we will ever need five Earths. As the demand for scarce resources rises, their price will increase. This should encourage people to use different resources and develop new technologies. But because we only have only one Earth, some people are suggesting another fix: find a new planet.

The solar system contains more resources than we could ever hope to use. Although space travel is extremely expensive now, it is quite possible that as technology improves, it will soon become efficient and effective to harvest asteroids for minerals, comets for water and even set up mines on the Moon.

Psyche 16 is an asteroid that lies between Mars and Jupiter. It is thought to be made entirely of metal – mostly iron, nickel and gold. The asteroid is estimated to be worth around $700,000,000,000,000,000,000,000. That is a fortune, enough to give each of the 7.6 billion people on Earth about $92 billion dollars each.

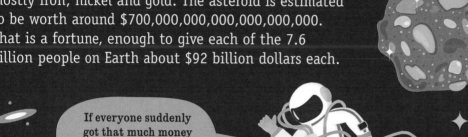

If everyone suddenly got that much money it would destroy the world economy.

Is moving to Mars a good idea?

The economic case for sending humans to Mars is a little harder to make. Because Mars is so far away it costs *a lot* to get there, especially if you need to carry things with you. There will always be cheaper ways to get resources from space.

But maybe that shouldn't stop us from trying. Although the original Moon landings didn't result in any permanent settlements (yet), the enormous investment in space exploration has produced many inventions that have made life on Earth better.

- solar panels
- hand-held vacuum cleaners
- memory-foam mattresses
- CAT scanners
- scratchproof glass
- wireless headphones
- in-ear thermometers

- laptop computers
- computer mouse
- LED bulbs
- water purifiers
- baby milk formula

So many questions...

Economists have considered many questions, some of which you might not even think count as economics. For example:

What's the best month of the year to be born in?

SEPTEMBER

In the northern hemisphere, if you were born in September, you are in luck. Researchers have discovered that September babies are more confident, more likely to get a college degree and the least likely to go to prison.

In most countries, the school year starts in September, so September babies are the eldest in their classes. Especially in the earliest years, that little age advantage can make a big difference and provide a lasting confidence boost.

I'm bigger and stronger than everyone else!

The same principle also applies to sports. Professional soccer players in Europe are much more likely to be born in January, for example, as January is the start month for age-levels in soccer.

In America, pro baseball players are more likely to be born in August for the same reason.

What causes famines?

When a town, region or country doesn't have enough food to feed its people, it's known as a **famine**. Indian economist Amartya Sen analyzed many famines and discovered something surprising.

Famines DON'T happen because there isn't enough food.

They happen because the price of food or labor changes – and people can't afford to feed their families any more.

People can starve even if plenty of food is being produced, as famines are usually caused by problems with food distribution.

Sen himself lived through a famine in Bengal in the 1940s. There, despite a better than average rice harvest, millions of people died. This was because laborer's wages couldn't keep up with rising food prices.

Sen was awarded the Nobel Prize for economics in 1998 for his ground-breaking work.

Should you stick to your first guess?

Studies have shown that in tests, 75% of students believe the first answer they think of is most likely to be right.

Unfortunately, they are *wrong*. One hundred years of experiments have demonstrated that people who trust the little voice in their head telling them to change their answers tend to improve their scores. Changes to answers are more likely to be from wrong to right, than the other way around.

The French revolution was in.... 1776?

Argh! Or was it 1789?

Why are Instagram influencers so successful?

Influencers are ordinary people who use social media to market their lifestyle and sell products. The influencer economy is worth BILLIONS of dollars worldwide.

Oddly, one of the main reasons for their success was discovered over a hundred years ago by an eccentric American economist named Theodore Veblen.

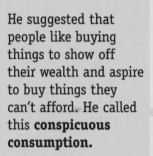

He suggested that people like buying things to show off their wealth and aspire to buy things they can't afford. He called this **conspicuous consumption.**

In the past, people were just trying to impress their neighbors – but on social media, successful influencers reach an audience of *millions*. Many businesses have recognized the advertising power that this brings.

Here's how influencing works:

Businesses often give an influencer expensive items for free.

£200

The influencer wears them in a video. Their fans see a person who seems pretty ordinary wearing cool, luxury glasses.

The fans want to copy the influencer. They buy a pair for themselves.

On the internet, an impulsive and expensive purchase is only a few clicks away. So be careful – and be aware that clever marketing is everywhere you look.

What gets left out?

Whether it's people deciding how to spend their money, businesses choosing who to hire, or governments trying to manage an economy, some people or things often get left out.

Informal markets

Some workers and businesses are invisible: they're not officially registered and they don't pay taxes. This makes it harder for the government to measure the economy, and they can't regulate these businesses and protect workers.

I'd like to grow this business, but I don't have a license from the government so I can't borrow money from the bank.

I work hard taking care of my baby, but nobody pays me for it.

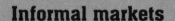

Women...

Ignoring certain groups can lead to governments making unfair decisions. For example, if the government cuts spending on pre-school education it tends to affect women more than men.

I'll have to stop working to look after Charlie.

...and race.

When people don't have the same opportunities, wages and rights because of their gender or race, it's known as **discrimination**.

I'm sorry, you're just not the right fit.

Is it because I don't look *like you?*

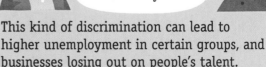

This kind of discrimination can lead to higher unemployment in certain groups, and businesses losing out on people's talent.

Banks

Until recently, economists often ignored banks when creating models of how a country's economy was working. Partly this was because banking is complicated, but mostly because they assumed banks, overall, simply get on with their job – helping people to save and borrow money. And this seemed to work until a banking crisis began in 2007 that affected the world economy.

Lots of American and European banks almost collapsed after taking huge risks and losing lots of money.

The banks stopped lending, businesses closed and people lost their jobs and homes.
There were recessions in many countries.

Economists struggled to make models of the consequences of the crisis and to suggest solutions.

Since then, economists have tried to model the risks banks can pose.

And governments have set rules to force banks to take fewer risks.

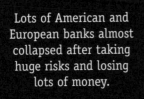

I need this wood.

Stop! We're working really hard for you!

Nature

It's easy to take the work nature does for granted, but *all* production depends on it for resources – and to turn waste *back into* resources. Here are some examples.

Trees turn polluted air into clean air.

Soil filters and cleans water, and allows most of our crops to grow.

Predators eat the bugs that destroy food crops.

If the way people consume and produce creates too much waste or uses too many resources, it threatens the work nature does *for* us. Economists call these externalities (see page 64) and are studying these "invisible" parts of the economy more and more.

Big questions

Some economists debate BIG questions such as 'What is a successful economy?' Here are some different answers.

I think a successful economy is one where people's basic needs are met *without* harming the planet. It looks a little like a donut.

British economist, Kate Raworth

Just right

Too little

The donut hole is the space where people's basic needs and rights aren't met.

Too much

If we put too much pressure on the environment, we end up outside the donut – dealing with problems such as water shortages.

I think the *richer* an economy is, and the higher its **GDP** is, the more successful it is.

Surely the *happiness* of people living there is more important than how much money a country has?

American economist, Richard Easterlin

Well, most things that make people happy cost money: parks, clean streets, good health...

But not all! Rich countries aren't necessarily the happiest and money isn't the only thing that makes people happy. Freedom to make choices, trust in governments, and supportive communities are all important too.

American economist, Betsey Stevenson

There isn't one right answer to this question. Often governments try to work towards all these definitions of a successful economy.

Small questions

Other economists focus on much smaller, more specific questions. In 2003, Indian and French economists Abhijit Banerjee and Esther Duflo helped set up Poverty Action Lab. The lab tests practical solutions to problems such as: How do you get more people to use mosquito nets to prevent them from getting malaria?

The PROBLEM: Malaria is a disease transmitted by infected mosquitoes. In 2017, there were 219 million cases and around 435,000 people died.

Sleeping under an insecticide-treated bed net is a really effective way of preventing malaria, but lots of people don't have one.

The QUESTION

What's the price which gets most people to use a net?

Free?

Are people more likely to use it if they've paid a tiny bit for it?

The Poverty Action Lab's approach is to look for **EVIDENCE** that a solution will actually work, before recommending it.

We're copying the main method doctors use to test medicines – randomized controlled trials. We set up this test so that similar people are randomly given a free net or one costing 60 cents.

We wonder if more people will choose to use a net if they have to pay for it, as it'll seem more valuable.

The TEST: In Kenya, to test how the price of a net affected how people used them, participants were randomly presented with option A...

...or option B.

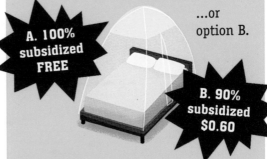

A. 100% subsidized FREE

B. 90% subsidized $0.60

The RESULT: 65% of people who were offered option A accepted it, compared to only 15% for option B. People used both nets just as much, whether they were free or not. So it was *actually* more efficient to give the nets out for free.

Making sense of the world

The world is big, changing and complicated. Economics is about finding ways of making sense of it. Here are some tips and techniques to help you do this, from using numbers to questioning facts.

Compare

It's hard to know how big or small a number is when it's by itself, so try to compare it to something else.

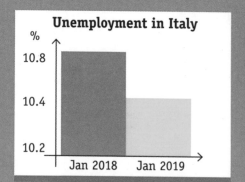

THE COURIER

KILLER CROCS GOBBLE 161 HUMANS IN 2017

This sounds scary, but compared to some other animals, crocodiles present very little risk to humans. Mosquitoes carrying diseases kill around **400,000** people each year.

Divide

One way of making a big number more meaningful is to divide it by a total – often the whole population. For example...

China produced 2,720 times more carbon emissions in 2017 than Iceland.

That's unacceptable, China must stop polluting the planet.

But when you divide it by the number of people in each country, China produces one and a half times less carbon emissions *per person* than Iceland does. This may change how you think of the problem.

Extreme scales

Unemployment in Italy

This graph makes it look like unemployment has halved in a year, but in fact it's dropped by just **0.4%**.

Missing or old data

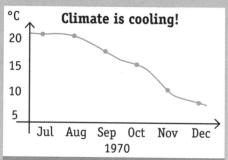

This graph shows the temperature cooling, but only for half the year from summer to winter, which is just what you'd expect. The data is also around 50 years old.

Be careful about making a **generalization**, or a broad statement about a group of people, things or countries.

Always check the facts before jumping to conclusions.

This is a very violent country. Every day, the news is full of criminals. We must spend more money on police officers.

Actually the crime rate is falling, and has been for the last 20 years.

Be ready to change your mind. This means you're open to new ideas; it doesn't mean you're easily led by others.

Actually, I think you'll find that the tooth fairy doesn't have to pay taxes.

How dare you disagree with me! I'm not friends with you any more.

It's because she uses money for charitable purposes.

Mmm, I hadn't thought of it that way.

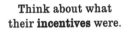

Don't blame people or businesses for their choices – find out *why* they made them.

Think about what their **incentives** were.

If you want to change their choices in the future, think about how to change their incentives.

If you don't change their incentives, they'll probably just make the same bad choice again.

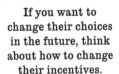

119

What next?

Economics is very complicated – but now you have the tools to understand it and start *using* it in your own life...

To hold politicians to account...

...and bamboozle your parents.

To understand difficult problems...

...and discuss how to fix them.

Glossary

This glossary explains some of the words used in this book.
Words written in *italic* type are explained in other entries.

capital anything that helps you *produce* things more efficiently, such as money, but also complex technology or even clever ideas.

capitalism an economic system in which private individuals and businesses control production rather than the government.

communism an economic system in which government takes control of production, with the belief that this will be fairer for everyone.

cost how much money a business spends on *production*.

demand how many people want to have something.

economy any community of people who consume, *produce* and *trade* things together.

externality a cost that is not borne by the producer but by the people around them. It is a market failure because the product's price doesn't reflect its true cost.

GDP Gross Domestic Product, the total amount of wealth generated by all the people and businesses in a country.

globalization the process of countries and businesses becoming more connected around the world.

incentive a reward that encourages people to make a particular choice.

inequality when some people or countries are wealthier, on average, than other people and countries.

inflation when prices for things go up over time and money loses value.

infrastructure road networks, power grids, police forces and other things that people in a community all rely on but rarely pay for directly.

interest an amount of money that people, businesses or governments agree to pay back to anyone they borrow money from, on top of the total amount borrowed.

interest rate a number, usually decided by the Federal Reserve, that tells lenders what amount of *interest* they are meant to charge.

labor *any* work that people do when *producing* something, whether it's physical work, thinking up ideas, or even telling other people what to do.

macroeconomics the study of choices that affect a whole country, or even the world.

market *any* place where people or businesses buy and sell things: from stores, to offices, to the internet.

market failure when something is unfair or unsafe for buyers or sellers in any *market*.

microeconomics the study of choices made by businesses, households and small *economies*.

mixed economy when governments *and* businesses produce things.

modeling using simplified versions of reality to test out ideas and find answers to questions.

monopoly when a single business controls a *market*.

oligopoly when just a few business control a market.

opportunity cost any choice a person makes means they've chosen not to do other things. The choices not taken are called an opportunity cost.

poverty when people do not have enough money to afford basic needs such as food and shelter.

production the process of making a *resource* into something, typically to *trade*.

profit the money gained by a business after *costs* are subtracted from *revenue*.

public services things provided for everybody by a government, paid through *taxes*.

regulation rules that governments set up to make markets work fairly, and to stop businesses from becoming too powerful.

resources anything people need to survive, and to use for *production*.

revenue the money a business earns by *producing* something.

scarcity the fact that there isn't enough of most *resources* and products to meet *demand*. It means that people have to make choices about what they want and how to share.

specialization when a person, business or country concentrates on *producing* some things and not others.

subsidy an *incentive*, in the form of money, paid by a government to people or businesses.

supply the amount of something available to be bought in a *market*.

surplus when a person, business or government has more of a *resource* or product than it needs.

tariff a tax that must be paid to a government if you want to sell a product in their country.

taxes money that individuals and businesses pay to the government

trade buying and selling *products* in a *market*.

trade war when two or more countries put up *tariffs* against each other's products.

trading bloc when two or more countries agree to share certain rules affecting their *markets*, such as shared *tariffs* or *regulations*.

unemployment the amount of people in an *economy* who don't have a job at a particular time.

utility a calculation of the value that people place on different choices.

Jobs in economics

Studying economics means trying to make sense of how lots of things work, from people to markets to governments. People who study economics often end up working in all sorts of jobs – many of them extremely well-paid, and some of them incredibly powerful.

accountant helps people keep track of exactly how much money they have earned, saved and spent – for individuals, businesses or even governments.

actuary determines how likely different events are to happen in the future, for example how long a person might live.

business development helps businesses and other organizations find ways to grow, and helps to improve relationships between businesses so they can all grow.

chief executive is in charge of running a business or organization.

civil servant works for governments to help them carry out policies and run the country efficiently.

data scientist researches all kinds of information, analyzes what that information contains, and presents it to people, for example to test how well *policies* are working.

economist studies economics, writes about economics, and often teaches it, too.

financial analyst studies markets, businesses and government regulations to predict what effects these will have.

forecasting analyst studies a particular industry, such as shipping, to determine how efficiently it could operate.

investment analyst studies markets and profits to help people and businesses decide how best to invest their money.

management consultant helps businesses and other organizations find ways to work more efficiently.

policy maker comes up with and tests ideas on how to make the world work better, or more fairly.

politician represents the opinions of people or of a political party, and turns policies into law. Around the world, many Presidents and Prime Ministers trained as economists.

quantity surveyor advises or oversees all levels of building projects.

stockbroker buys and sells stocks and shares at a stock exchange on behalf of clients, as well as advising clients on what to buy or sell.

Index

Acknowledgements

Written by
Andy Prentice & Lara Bryan

Illustrated by
Federico Mariani

Edited by
Alex Frith

Designed by Jamie Ball
& Freya Harrison

Economics experts:
David Stallibrass,
First Principles Economics
Pedro Serôdio,
University of Middlesex

Series editor: Jane Chisholm
American editor: Carrie Armstrong

Series designer:
Stephen Moncrieff